BLACK GOLD

BLACK GOLD

Nuggets
from a Lifetime of Laughs

Arthur Black

HARBOUR PUBLISHING

Harbour Publishing Co. Ltd.
P.O. Box 219
Madeira Park, BC V0N 2H0
www.harbourpublishing.com

Cover photography by Howard Fry
Printed and bound in Canada

Harbour Publishing acknowledges financial support from the Government of Canada through the Book Publishing Industry Development Program and the Canada Council for the Arts, and from the Province of British Columbia through the BC Arts Council and the Book Publishing Tax Credit.

THE CANADA COUNCIL | LE CONSEIL DES ARTS
FOR THE ARTS | DU CANADA
SINCE 1957 | DEPUIS 1957

BRITISH
COLUMBIA
ARTS COUNCIL
Supported by the Province of British Columbia

Library and Archives Canada Cataloguing in Publication

Black, Arthur

    Black gold : nuggets from a lifetime of laughs / Arthur Black.

Also available in audiobook format.

ISBN 1-55017-373-1

    1. Canadian wit and humor (English). I. Title.

PS8553.L318B5195 2006   C818'.5402   C2006-903339-0

For Bernie Slade, who said,
"a laugh is the reverse of a breakdown;
it's a breakup."

Contents

Introduction

Another damned thick, square book!
Always scribble, scribble, scribble, eh, Mr. Gibbon?

I love that quote. I can picture William, Duke of Gloucester (I see him as Ralph Klein in a periwig), face flushed and spittle flying, rounding on poor Mr. Gibbon, who has had the temerity to offer the Duke a copy of his just-published opus. The year is 1781. The book is volume two of Gibbon's *History of the Decline and Fall of the Roman Empire*. It is as seminal a work as any mortal could hope to pen, still famous nearly two and a half centuries after it was written, but to the Duke it's just "scribble, scribble, scribble."

Not surprisingly, my sympathies lie with Mr. Gibbon. I, too, have been scribble, scribble, scribbling—in my case, for the past four decades. I've scribbled for newspapers, magazines, television and radio. Tomorrow I shall scribble some more.

Do I do it for the glory? The fabulous paydays? The thrill of fending off coveys of adoring fans? No, no and no. The CanLit scene is notably deficient in the glory and adoration departments. As for the paydays, I probably would have made more as a house painter. I scribbled my way through life for two reasons: to pay the rent and because I was no good at anything else. I'm a mechanical klutz, a mathematical cretin and a hapless mook at office politics and business procedure in general.

Well, make it three reasons. I love the sound of human laughter. I don't care if it's a chuckle or cackle, snigger or snicker, a wheeze, a snort, a titter, a crow, a hoot or one of those great rolling belly laughs that simultaneously threaten suffocation and incontinence.

I love to make people merry. I've written eleven books with no greater purpose in mind. *Black Gold* is a collection of my favourite pieces from those books.

It's no *Decline and Fall*, but it's definitely good for a laugh. I think even the Duke of Gloucester would have enjoyed it.

—ARTHUR BLACK, 2006

Basic Black

1981

Cross-Country Skiing

I would like to say a few words about a disease. A particular brand of madness that has infested our nation from coast to coast.

Well . . . I don't know that it's *that* far gone. I can't testify for exotic spas like Victoria and Musquadobit Harbour. Perhaps the citizenry of Tuktoyaktuk and Point Pelee have more sense. But for the most part, any place in the country that can hold an inch or two of snow on the ground for more than twenty-four hours will be suffering in some measure from this strange affliction.

Cross-country skiing is what I'm talking about. You may know it as touring or nordic skiing. A ruse by any other name. They are all devious euphemisms for the same senseless pastime.

Cross-country skiing is basically jogging while wearing lumber. The same personality type that would make mock of a summer morning by donning pyjamas with a racing stripe, forty-dollar sneakers and lurching around a football field until his lungs burst— that's the kind of bedrock lunatic who is the very foundation of cross-country madness.

The cross-country fanatic is not to be confused with the downhiller. Cross-country is kind of the poor-but-proud hillbilly cousin of decadent downhill. Anyone who is rich, beautiful and brainless enough to look comfortable in a Canadian beer commercial usually gravitates toward the Downhill scene with its astronaut accoutrements and the après-ski perks of crackling logs in the fireplace, hot toddies and dancing chic to chic in form-fitting Eddie Bauer down-filled vests. When all that's going down at the chalet, you can sometimes look out the floor-to-ceiling thermopane and occasionally catch just a flicker of the cross-country skier . . . shuffling sullenly among the spruce trees.

Contrary to what you might have heard . . . cross-country skiing is easy. You just shuffle with your feet and stab with your poles. Fall down, get up. Shuffle, stab, fall down . . . get up, get cold, shuffle, stab, turn around, shuffle, stab, fall down, get up, shuffle, stab, back to your car. Take off the skis and go home. In cross-country, the skiing part is childishly simple. It's the *choosing* you have to do that makes it difficult.

First the skis. You will spend your first ski season fretting over what kind of skis you should have bought rather than the ones you did. There are wooden skis, wooden skis with lignite edges, skis with wood bottoms and plastic tops . . . plastic skis, and finally *really* plastic skis—skis with ripples and dimples on the bottom that are supposed to make the perverse science of waxing unnecessary.

Needless to say, any cross-country purist sneers at waxless skis. What? Ski and not wax? It's like asking Glenn Gould to sit down at a player piano.

I'm here to tell you that waxless skis work perfectly. Whenever you achieve a precise combination of sun and temperature and age of snow and condition of track—which is to say, perhaps three outings in a lifetime.

But that's okay . . . because that's about how often you'll hit the right ski wax if you go with the slats that need waxing.

Ever checked out cross-country waxes? The sales clerk will tell you you only need three, really—green for cold, blue for not too cold and red for warm . . . but then you'll be tempted to round out your kit with a pale green for very cold, a purple for those not quite blue and not yet red days . . . and before you know it you'll have a packsack full of emeralds, indigos, chartreuses, violets and a whole herd of maverick waxes including yellow, black, orange and so help me, silver.

You think I jest? Lemme read to you from a random collection of waxes I have here. Here's a piquant little brown that I think you'll find amusing: Instructions on the tube: "For dry new snow, 18° F. and below . . . thin layer. From 18 to 30⁰ F.—thicker layer . . . smooth out well."

Here's another tube—a zesty cerulean blue—it reads: "For fine grained snow from minus one Celsius to minus five Celsius . . . and fresh snow from minus one Celsius to minus three Celsius . . . polish to a fine film" blah blah . . . I've got an even funnier one in a black tube but unfortunately the instructions read: "Ranta ja nuos-kalin Lempe leppanen, sisu quitos suomi kovisto sibelius" and so on . . . that's one of the features of cross-country waxes—they come like lipstick, with the instructions printed on the side—only you have to peel away the container as you use the wax. First peel takes out the English instructions and you are left with Finnish, Norwegian, Lapp and occasionally Russian—but that's a whole other fault report. No . . . the point is, by the time you've decided whether the snow is fresh or old, fine or coarse, dry or wet, fluffy or granular . . . and decided whether you should polish to a fine layer or lay it on like peanut butter . . . by the time you've done all this in the middle of the bush on a midwinter day, your feet are cold, your hands are numb and anyway it's time to go home.

And yet it goes on. Phenomenally. It's more and more popular every year—there are marathon ski tours right across the country that attract thousands of entrants each. The Canadian Ski Marathon held recently in Quebec made tourers ski more than 100 miles in terrible terrain over two days. The wind chill factor on opening day made for a temperature of something like fifty below. Four thousand people entered!

Why? Who knows? I guess it's one way to beat Canada's rotten winters . . . Gives you the illusion that you're meeting winter on its own terms and all that Jack London stuff.

Met one marathoner who says he skis every day in the winter to avoid getting cabin fever.

Poor devil. Either his brain is raddled with klister fumes or he's just too far gone to reason.

Doesn't realize that cross-country skiing *is* cabin fever. On runners.

Ringette

Okay sports fans . . . you think you've got your stats down pat? Think you're a walking Encyclopedia of Sweat because you know the Blue Jays' pitching staff by heart? Because you know without looking it up who won the Grey Cup where and from who in 1953? Because your depth of hockey savvy is so profound you know that Sheldon Kanageiser was an NHL defenceman not an Israeli hors d'oeuvre? Think ya know everything you need to know about sports, eh? Okay, here's a soft lob for you . . . what's Canada's very own game?

Hockey? Hah. If the Russians and Swedes haven't disproved that for you recently, check out a painting by Pieter Brueghel the Elder called *The Return of the Hunters*. Among other things in that painting you will note several rink ratty-looking youngsters scooting around a sheet of ice swatting at a disc with their curved sticks. Not exactly Philadelphia Flyer hopefuls perhaps, but shinny players by any other name. The painting was done in 1565.

Lacrosse? Well, you can make a better case for that. Back in the 1700s French explorers noticed that many North American Indian tribes liked to play a game they called Baggitaway with hooped, thonged sticks and a hard leather sphere. The French called it *le jeu de la crosse* and promptly stole it—which as far as I'm concerned, invalidates it as an invention belonging to Canada. Lacrosse is a First

Nations game that was being played centuries before arenas dotted a country called Canada.

Nope. The English have cricket and the Yanks have baseball and the Scots have golf, the Cubans have jai alai and the Scandinavians have cross-country skiing and Canada . . .

Well, Canada has Ringette.

Yup. Ringette. It's ours. Not just Canadian, but northern Ontarian. And young. Invented by a North Bay Parks and Recreation Director back in 1965. As the suffix on the word would indicate, Ringette is strictly for girls . . . and at the moment it's as close as young girls can get to the sport their brothers are involved in all winter—ice hockey. Ringette, for those who have never seen a game, is played on ice. The players carry bladeless sticks and use a donut-style ring instead of a puck. Unlike the animal house antics that frequently ruin ice hockey, there is no such thing as goon-style Ringette. No body contact is allowed. No sticks can be raised above the shoulder.

Well, Ringette is not even twenty years old—is it thriving? Yes and no. Something like sixty thousand Canadians now play the game, more than half of them in Ontario. Sixty thousand participants certify Ringette as something more than a northern Ontario eccentricity—as a matter of fact there are Ringette enclaves in the US, the Soviet Union and Czechoslovakia. But it's a long way from becoming a regular feature of the winter Olympics.

Personally I think the game suffers from terminal cuteness. Ringette terminology is patronizing as hell and would give Gloria Steinem or Germaine Greer palpitations. Divisions like Petite, Tween, Junior, Belle, and Debs sound suffocatingly patronizing— even the name of the game sounds like a Toni home permanent you'd give your Barbie Doll. Ringette.

However, silly names have never doomed a sport. Look at cricket. Spelunking. Squash. Curling. Snooker.

If for some reason it doesn't survive, though, I'd like to point out that Canadians shouldn't feel totally bereft. One Canadian sports innovation I neglected to mention was the one that's made household names of beanpoles like Wilt the Stilt, Meadowlark and Kareem Abdul-Jabbar.

Basketball. We invented it. Or at least a Canadian did. Doctor James Naismith, when he was teaching at the YMCA college down in Springfield, Massachussetts, back in 1891.

I know, I know . . . all you sports stats fanatics out there who can recite the won-lost-tied tallies of the old Birmingham Bulls before breakfast—you guys are ready to jump on that one. Basketball wasn't invented in 1891 you're sneering—the Aztecs were playing basketball back when Pieter Breughel was painting fifteenth-century forwards.

Well not exactly. The Aztecs played an almost unpronounce-able game called Ollamalitzli, which involved throwing a ball (solid) through a stone ring, which jutted out high on one wall of a stadium. But the stakes were a little higher than your average NBA match.

The player who put the ball through the ring was entitled to all the clothes of the spectators. The captain of the losing team, was expected to offer his head for his sins.

I don't think your average multi-million dollar basketball super-star would much care for stakes like that.

Don't think modern spectators would be too crazy about it either.

It's one thing to lose a few bucks on a match. But coming home naked?

Borders

would like to direct your attention to a curious Canadian ritual.

Well, it's not exactly a ritual so much as a whole new growth industry. You've probably noticed the salesmen. They're thundering all around this dominion right now—self-appointed saviours of the nation . . . beating the bushes, checking under mattresses, peering into attics and root cellars, storm sewers and subway tunnels . . . winnowing out the precious links and nuggets that . . . HOLD THIS NATION TOGETHER. "What makes us special?" they ask (usually rhetorically) . . . "What cuts Canadians apart from the rest of the human herd?"

They come up with all kinds of answers: Ookpik. Anne Murray. The Precambrian Shield. Poutine.

But to my mind, they've all overlooked the most precious and obvious strand of Canadiana there is. What makes Canadians distinct from every other race, creed or nation state? What cements the incredible tossed salad of nationalities and ethnic strains that make up this great nation of ours?

What indeed, if not that one mind-boggling ceremony . . . that one knee-trembling, stomach-flopping sacrament that every Canadian past toddling age observes . . . sometimes just once, often twice or even several times a year?

The Border Crossing.

Doesn't matter where in Canada you live. You can cross the border at Ogdensburg, New York, or Coutts, Alberta; Niagara Falls or New Westminster; Dawson in the Yukon or Calais down in Maine . . . doesn't matter a jot. Point is: you're Canadian . . . so you'll do it. It's just one of the things you're expected to do as a Canadian. Everybody goes "down to the States." It's tradition, eh?

God knows why. For many years, when the Canadian dollar was worth a nickel or so more than its American cousin, I think Canadians just went down to the States to feel smug.

Wasn't much reason other than that. True, Havana cigars were cheaper down there, but our cigarettes were stronger, our beer got you drunk quicker, and if you asked for vinegar with your chips, American waitresses checked to see if you were wearing a plastic bracelet and a hunted look.

And the other thing that made—and makes—going down to the States about as sensible as the lemmings' mass swan dive—is the border crossing itself. Not so much going down to the States . . . as coming BACK from the States . . . when you come face to face with the full majesty of Canada Customs. It's eerie. Somewhere between the sign that says: "Thanks fer comin'. Y'all come back!" and the one that frigidly announces "Douane Canada Customs" . . . you begin to feel a gnawing uncertainty . . . an uncertainty that swells to a paranoid conviction that you will never actually get to walk on your homeland again. Except maybe in the exercise yard as a convicted felon.

Think about the last time you crossed the border. Have you ever been more terrified? Can you recall a time when any Canadian official was more offhand with you? Or a time when you acted like such a wimp in response?

Ah yes . . . It's always the same with the Border Crossing. What complicates the problem of course is that Canada is a nation of amateur smugglers. Not heroin-in-the-rocker-panel type smugglers. More like Marlboros in the Glove Compartment.

Now come on . . . don't blush. You're not the only one who ever ran the border with an Omega digital on a flexible Speidel band cutting off the circulation in your upper forearm. And you're not the first one to have his entire life flash before his eyes when the lantern-jawed, tight-lipped gent with Canada Customs emblazoned on his bulging shoulder leaned in to cast an insolent eye over everything in your back seat.

Where do they get the questions? Where do they get *the delivery?*

"AFTNOON... YOU Λ CNAJUN CITZEN PRESNTLY RESIDING WTHIN BORDERS OF WHICH PROVINCE NOW... YOURE BORN WHERE... HAVE YOUEVER BEEN CNVICTED OF INDICTABLE OFFENCE'R' FRANY REASON RFUSED PMISSION TCROSS BORDER... YOU MAAM WHERE D'YOU WORK... THIS YOUR CHILD CARRYIN ANY BEERWINESPIRITS OR FIRE-ARMS EVER CONSORTED WITH KNOWN TERRORISTS ARE YOU PRESENTLY EMPLOYED HOW MANY TRANS BORDER TRIPS 'VYOU MADE THIS CALENDAR QUARTER ANY REPAIRS MADE TO THIS VEE HICLE AND HOW LONG HAVE YOU BEEN OUT OF CANADA?"

And just when you were ready to ransom your spouse, leave your firstborn as security and babble a confession about the bottle of bourbon under the car blankct... He writes something cryptic on a notepad and waves you through.

What does it mean? Are they waiting to see if your nerve will break? Will Mounties be waiting in your driveway? Will plain-clothesmen come to the office six months hence to drag you away? Who knows? It's all part of the larger mystery of The Crossing... The crossing of the great undefended border. Ah yes... If all the guff that's been written about the magnificence and nobility of that 5,000-mile-long checkout counter was piled in one row... we'd have a barrier that would make the Great Wall of China look like a picket fence. Somebody once referred to our border as: "that long frontier from the Atlantic to the Pacific Ocean, guarded only by neighbourly respect and honourable obligations."

Respect? Honour? It is to whimper brokenly. The somebody who said that about our border was one Winston Churchill, in a speech at the Canada Club in London, back during the Second World War.

Mister Churchill had crossed the border perhaps once. And then with all the pomp and splendour, not to mention brandy and cigars, that go with being the world popular PM of a Mother Country at war.

All the same. Winnie was a canny old codger.

I like to think that when he crossed the border from the US into Canada . . . and the usually supercilious customs people turned obsequious in a flurry of salutes and applause . . . I like to think that if you'd been standing just behind Winnie when he doffed his homburg in return . . . you'd have caught just a flash of a half dozen or so hand-rolled Havanas . . . securely Scotch-taped to the inside of the crown.

Siestas

Somebody once described a Canadian as: "someone who drinks Brazilian coffee from an English teacup and munches a French pastry while sitting on his Danish furniture, having just come home from an Italian movie in his German car. He picks up his Japanese pen and writes to his member of Parliament to complain about the American takeover of the Canadian publishing business."

Yep, we're a great nation of carpers, not to mention borrowers . . . but while we were cruising about the far-flung flea markets and discount houses of the world . . . it really is a pity that we didn't pick up one bargain-basement buy . . . the siesta.

The siesta . . . what a thoroughly civilized idea. You know how it works? Actually, "works" is the wrong word. Siestas are about *not* working. A three-hour break in the middle of the working day, when the hard, harried, jangling world of commerce and industry screeches to a halt and everyone . . . *relaxes.*

A delicious bite-sized chunk of the best part of the day reserved for rest and recreation. No scurrying to banks or haring around the aisles of a supermarket either, because the people that make the banks and supermarkets work are taking a siesta too. Bank managers take siestas. Checkout girls take siestas. The siesta is nothing if not democratic.

And we don't have it. They have it in Spain. They have it in Italy. They have it in Portugal and parts of South and Central America. But we don't have it here. And it's our loss. Think of what you could do with three uninterrupted quiet hours in the middle of the working day. Next time you're levering open your lunch box to get at those cold baloney sandwiches, or lining up beside that squalid little lunch wagon in the parking lot—the one that sells pressed cardboard sandwiches and plastic wrapped honey buns and styrofoam cups of mud with cream and sugar . . . reflect for a moment that your counterpart in Spain or Italy . . . The Madrileño and the Venetian and the Roman worker . . . is sitting down at home to a sumptuous midday meal, with a glass of wine and bambinos gathered round . . . secure in the knowledge that work is three full hours away. Must be nice. Mind you it might not be nice much longer. Indications are that the fine old tradition of the siesta is under serious assault in Rome right now.

There are a number of prongs in the attack—rising gas prices and horrible traffic congestion make it more difficult and expensive to get from plant or office to home each midday . . . then too, siesta-takers have noticed that their habit has an unavoidably inflationary effect on the waistline. Trade unions are clamouring for a shorter workday, and the easiest way to make it shorter would be to squeeze out that little three-hour vacuum in the middle of the workday sandwich. But most serious of all, it seems that Rome has caught a fairly severe case of the Anglo Saxon disease.

That's the one you and I suffer from. Nine to five-ism. Efficiency. Productivity. All those horrible words that cost-effectiveness types keep throwing at us . . . words that should never have been applied to anything more animated than a Husquevarna chainsaw or a Massey-Ferguson combine.

But I'm not worried. The siesta has been under siege for centuries. Ever since some peasant in the dim and distant past drew the obvious conclusion that only an idiot would work in the heat of the midday, tilted his sombrero over his nose and went to sleep, there have been petty tyrants and would-be foremen nattering at him to wake up, shape up, roll up his sleeves and get on out there and win one for El Gipper. Newspaper editorials in Spain have railed against the siesta almost as long as they've railed against bullfights.

Successive Italian governments have promised that one of their first reforms would be abolition of the siesta. I have a theory that's why there've been so *many* successive Italian governments. People don't want their siesta messed with.

And rightly so. The siesta is a People's Movement in the purest sense of the word. Or non-movement I suppose.

Siestas are for us. For families. For lovers. For reading good books and eating fine meals. For good conversation. For a glass of wine. For looking at trees and for listening to birds.

Remember the line: "A loaf of bread, a jug of wine and thou . . ." You think that was written in the measly hour between blasts of a factory whistle? Uh uh. That's siesta talk.

Remember, too, the line: "Mad dogs and Englishmen go out in the midday sun."

So do Canadians. And more's the pity.

Back to Black

1987

Swimming in the Elora Quarry

Ever gone for a swim in a quarry? To me, it's one of the most delightful treats you can give your body. With water, anyway. There's something about the clarity of the water and the towering limestone walls that makes quarry swimming highly sensual. Especially if you deck yourself out with snorkel and face mask and dip into the beautiful world below the surface.

Or perhaps it's just a personal fetish. After all, I learned to swim in a rock quarry when I was a mere guppy, several hundred years ago. The Elora Quarry, it was . . . a magnificent crater in the landscape between the southern Ontario towns of Elora and Fergus. The Elora Quarry is—well, heck, I don't know how big it is, but it's big. Wide enough that my arms turn to spaghetti when I try to swim across. And the distance from the lip of the quarry to the dancing blue-green water far below is such that I take a deep breath before I even peer over the side. As for the daredevil teenagers who actually leap off the cliffs, even they wear sneakers to absorb the smack of their feet hitting the water. Those kids don't have to worry about touching bottom. The water in the quarry is thirty feet deep, so there's really no danger.

Providing they survive the fall.

Jumping off the side of the Elora Quarry has never been my idea of a fun pastime, and there's no need anyway. There's a gently sloping path for we lesser breeds who wish to sample the water without having a mid-air coronary.

I remember the first time I walked that path. I can still feel the sharp limestone gravel under my six-year-old feet. I remember timidly entering the water and that first, terrifying thrill when the bottom drops away and you begin to flail and you realize that you are *swimming*.

Or in my case, sinking.

Ah, but I bobbed up eventually, spluttering and choking and gasping for air, but doing a kind of frenzied, instinctive dog paddle that got my mouth above the waterline every once in a while. Before that afternoon was over, I'd even learned to thrash my way from one point to another. I was no threat to Johnny Weissmuller or Esther Williams, but I was "swimming," after a fashion.

Since that day, I've swam in quarries all over Ontario. I've also tried them in Spain and Italy and Mexico. In Mexico they're called *cenotes* and they occur naturally, but swimming in a *cenote* feels just as exquisite as it does in an Ontario rock quarry.

They were all very nice . . . but only because they reminded me of the Elora Quarry. I always dreamed that one day I would swim and snorkel there again. Last spring, after a quarter of a century's absence, I moved back to the Fergus-Elora area. The quarry I'd dreamed about is just a couple of miles down the road. Last week I went back for a swim.

I discovered, à la Rip Van Winkle, that there have been some changes. The rambling cowpath that used to lead from the highway to the quarry is gone. It's been replaced by a large, paved parking lot. There's a concession stand hawking soft drinks, french fries and hot dogs. As kids we used to pedal to the quarry on our CCMs and not see another soul all day. Now there's a toll booth and it costs a dollar fifty for adults and fifty cents for kids. There are concrete pillbox washrooms, litter buckets and conservation officers every few feet. Before I got ten paces from my car I was nailed by one of the Quarry Guardians who told me, with a Happy Face smile, that the snorkel, mask and fins under my arm were *verboten*.

"Why?" I asked.

"No floating objects allowed," she smiled.

No problem, I smiled back, pointing out that my mask, snorkel and fins would, if left unattended, sink like stones. The only floating object would—hopefully—be me.

She upped the wattage on her smile and hit me with the classic Eichmann Defence, "I'm sorry, but I don't make the rules."

So there I was, standing beside my beloved Elora Quarry, surrounded by leering conservation officers determined to crush any criminal activity I might have in mind. I looked around. Sure enough, there wasn't a face mask, snorkel or swim fin to be seen. Just ghetto blasters, teeny boppers, crushed dixie cups and the acrid, bitter-sweet aroma of a Controlled Substance burning nearby.

I kept trying to conjure up that Norman Rockwellish vignette of tousle-haired, freckle-faced lads on a hot summer afternoon, dangling their feet in the water. But it was difficult. Especially with Madonna screeching "Material Girls" from a suitcase radio just off my starboard earhole.

Ah, I tell ya . . . sometimes it's tough being an old fogey.

Ersatz Deer and Stonehenge

Once I took my kids to Disneyworld in Florida. It wasn't too bad till we got on a little train for a ride through—I don't know . . . one of those time warp suburbs in the land of Mickey and Donald and Goofy. Frontierland, I think it was. We chugged slowly past a lot of American historical mockups while a man with a microphone told us what we were seeing. Off in the distance, right by a painted river, stood a herd of whitetail deer. That's what the man said they were. Even fifty feet away they looked distressingly fake. Rigid, glassy-eyed, their polystyrene antlers bobbing up and down robotically in a bad imitation of browsing. They were to living deer as Howdy Doody is to Rudolf Nureyev.

Which would have been okay for the kids I suppose. Except none of the kids around me paid any attention to the deer herd. No—it was the adults! Adults were snapping pictures like paparazzi at a photo opportunity with a porn star.

I was reminded of those ersatz whitetails as I read a story out of England a while back.

You know Stonehenge—that remarkable and mysterious formation of massive rocks on Salisbury Plain? It's been standing there for thirty-five hundred years while people played guessing games about it. It's been called a religious altar, a solar calendar, a lunar observatory, an astronomical computer, and a marker buoy for extra terrestrials. Truth is, we don't know precisely what Stonehenge is or why it was built. But we do know that it's man-made. That somehow, prehistoric humans quarried unthinkably huge rocks—some weighing fifty tons—then somehow dragged and hauled and pushed and levered them up to twenty miles from the quarry to erect them in complex and largely undecipherable patterns at what we call Stonehenge.

An amazing achievement—and one that has drawn tourists to the otherwise unremarkable Salisbury Plain for hundreds of years. In fact, six hundred thousand curious people visit Stonehenge every year.

And that's the problem. Too many tourists visiting Stonehenge. They've climbed and mauled and sometimes chipped away chunks of the monoliths. Some idiots have done a Kilroy Was Here with spray bombs and chalk, and even chisels. But even the passive spectators do damage. Archaeologists say the very pounding of thousands of pairs of feet on the ground around the stones threatens the future of the site.

So what to do? Restrict the number of visitors? Give them all a crash course in archaeological etiquette? Close the site entirely?

They have, believe it or not, come up with something more bizarre than that. The officials are talking of... plasticizing Stonehenge. Honest to God. The suggestion is that they close the site entirely and erect a fibreglass replica of Stonehenge somewhere else. Right now they're looking at the possibility of setting up an imitation, exact-scale Stonehenge in a nearby safari park.

Well, I say why just move it down the road? Why not make it really convenient and relocate in downtown London close to all the big hotels? How about Hyde Park? You could call it Clonehenge.

Which reminds me again of that Disneyworld deer herd I started out talking about. Guy next to me on the Frontierland train was practically screwing his Nikon into his head he was taking so many shots of the deer herd. "Where ya from?" I asked him while he was changing film. "Wisconsin," he said. "You don't have deer in Wisconsin?" I asked. "Sure we do," he said. "But they don't stay still like this in Wisconsin."

Send the Shoes Out by Themselves

I have never been a big fan of the whole concept of Extreme Exertion. For human beings, I mean. I have no quarrel with race-horses, cheetahs, peregrine falcons or Aston Martins that want to race flat out until their little piston-driven hearts burst. That is their choice. I won't stand in their way.

The same goes for joggers. I happen to believe privately that jogging is the dumbest way of spending your time this side of live grenade juggling, but that's all right. To each his own.

I prefer to stand at my living room window with something tall, cold and liver-threatening in my left hand, using my right to encourage the joggers as they lurch past my driveway. We also serve who only stand and wave.

I used to feel guilty about my hostility toward the Sweaty Sports, but less and less as time goes on. And this month alone, there have been three major developments in the field of sports that convince me that the thoroughfare marked "Sloth and Lethargy" is the only dual highway worth travelling.

The first sign was the beeping centre field fence. The Japanese (of course) have come up with a baseball fence that beeps. It's a kind of sonar system for fielders to warn them as they float back to get under a fly ball that they are in danger.

As soon as they get close to the old fence: BWEEP BWEEP BWEEP BWEEP.

I suppose outfielders with depth perception problems will rush to endorse the beeping fence, but I don't see it as a giant leap forward for the game. Like the aluminum bat and artificial turf it just makes the game a little more predictable and a little less human.

The second sports innovation to hit the news recently comes from Wilsons' Sporting Goods. It is the oversize tennis ball. Why would anyone want an oversize tennis ball? Because it has more wind resistance of course, which makes it travel slower. Says one player who has tried the tumescent tennis ball, "If your opponent is overpowering you, this ball cuts down his advantage."

Well, I suppose. And if the bigger ball doesn't improve your game you could always give your opponent a flesh wound in his serving arm.

Ah, but it's the third athletic breakthrough that really caught my imagination. Frankly, I'm surprised joggers got along without it until now. I refer, of course, to the revolutionary footwear soon to be available from Puma shoes—the RS Shoe—the first jogging shoe that is, as they say, computer compatible. Yep, now you can come in from your morning run, peel off your soggy sweats and just before you hop in the shower, plug your Pumas into your Apple or Commodore.

By the time you're towelling down, you'll be able to scan your very own printout, detailing how many miles you ran, how long it took you and how many calories you burned up doing it. Ain't progress wonderful? You bet your aerobically enhanced cardiovascular system it is.

But why stop now? Beeping baseball fences are fine, but why not go the extra step? Why not put baseballs on long elastics so they can't threaten outfielders' decorum by being hit out of the park? Let's play tennis with Nerf balls so everybody gets an equal chance. As for the Puma computerized jogging shoe . . . hey. Why jeopardize a perfectly sound piece of technological wizardry by allowing a human foot to stomp all over it? Send the shoes out *by themselves* for your morning run. They can be programmed to come home and plug themselves into the computer. Let's face it. If you're not *in* the shoes, slowing them down, your time can only improve.

Besides, that way you could join me at the living room window to watch your Pumas jog by while we have a couple of drinks. I'm buying.

Fairytales on Trial

That old American curmudgeon, H.L. Mencken, once defined a courtroom as: "a place where Jesus Christ and Judas Iscariot would be equals . . . with the betting odds in favour of Judas."

I was thinking about Mr. Mencken as I read a news story about a circuit court trial that took place down in Madison, Wisconsin recently. The defendant was being tried in absentia, but she was found guilty of criminal trespass, damage to property, and theft.

Theft of porridge. The jury was made up of a bunch of first- and second-grade school kids. The defendant was one Goldilocks. The whole thing was an exercise to demonstrate to youngsters the full majesty of the legal system. A laudable idea I suppose . . . but what really caught my eye was the defence mounted by the lawyer —all three and one-half feet of her—representing Goldilocks. The lawyer argued that there had been "a classic misunderstanding between her client and the Bear Family." Goldilocks, she said, had only entered the bears' domain because she had been chased by a swarm of bees.

Ladies and gentlemen of the jury, I submit that this is one defence attorney who does not have all that much more to learn about the legal system in North America. She's already mastered lesson number one: when in doubt, stickhandle.

I predict ripe pickings for this miniature Melvin Belli as she strides through the juicy litigational hunting grounds of Hans Christian Andersen, Lewis Carroll and the Brothers Grimm. She'll probably represent the suffering mother in *Alice in Wonderland*. Mental anguish—contributing to the delinquency of a minor (remember those card games?) and trafficking in a controlled substance (magic mushrooms). They could also sue the owner of that hole—call it an uncovered well—that Alice fell down. Hit him for every cent he's got.

What about Hansel and Gretel? Nobody's ever looked at that fable from the Witch's point of view. It would be a posthumous suit of course, the Witch finishing up as she did doing a slow burn in her own oven. But it's a cornerstone of our judicial system that you don't lose your rights just because you're dead. The way I see it, Hansel and Gretel, their heirs and dependants are wide open for a monster lawsuit on the grounds of trespass, unpaid-for lodging and, for those nibbles they took out of the gingerbread wainscotting—theft under $200. Not to mention first-degree witchslaughter of course.

Lots of potential pigeons for the plucking in folklore. The woodsman in *Little Red Riding Hood*—get him for break and entry and carrying an unregistered weapon. Cinderella could do time for impersonating royalty . . .

Snow White? She's tough because she's . . . well, snow white. But the Seven Dwarfs? A goldmine. Kidnapping, unlawful confinement and failure to pay the minimum wage just for starters.

Oh yes. The Three Little Pigs for littering; Humpty Dumpty for loitering; Peter Pan for piloting a substandard aircraft . . . the possibilities are endless. And I can't understand why the legal profession had to wait for a Grade 2 defence attorney from Madison, Wisconsin to point the way. After all, lawyers have never been shy about peeling new plums before.

Reminds me of the story of two burglars holding a whispered conference outside a jimmied window. One burglar has just come out of the house. The other is standing watch.

"Did ja get anything?" rasps the sentry.

"Nah, nothin," says the other. "A lawyer lives here."

"Jeez, that's too bad," says the first. "Ja lose anything?"

Great Moments at the Bar

Sometimes when I get weary of the writing business, I fantasize about returning to one of my previous labour incarnations. I've got lots to choose from. I've been a movie extra and a sheet metal apprentice; I've herded cattle at the stock yards, loaded trucks in a food terminal, taught English and unclogged drains; I've sprayed paint on to the walls of school gymnasiums and I've chipped paint off the decks of an oil tanker; I've acted as a tour guide and I've stooked hay . . . and I've sold: encyclopedias, men's wear, newspaper advertising. For most of those jobs, once in a lifetime is more than ample . . . and time has not rosied my assessment. But there is one job from my past that beckons alluringly every once in a while. It was a job I held down when I was working my way through—okay, halfway through—college. Okay, not college—Ryerson Polytechnic in Toronto.

The job was bartending. Yup, I tended a bar in downtown Toronto for . . . I guess the best part of two years. I was a curly-haired, apple-cheeked innocent of eighteen summers when I started. I had grown up, for the most part, in the suburbs. *Leave It to Beaver* country where everybody washed their cars and clipped their lawns and smiled a lot and voices were only raised in songs around the barbecue or if some kid on the school team hit a home run. And I went from that *Ozzie and Harriet* land to a bar in downtown Toronto.

It was educational. Multiculturally enlightening. The head bartender, for instance, was Gus the Greek. "BRRRINGUE ME TWO CAYSA FEEFTEY, WAN AH CANADEEN, A CASE OFF EGGSPORT Den SHADDAPA DOAN BODDAH ME."

That was Gus the Greek's standard sign-off. You knew the message was complete when he got to Shaddapa Doan Boddah Me! For him it was Roger, Ten-Four Over and Out.

Then there was Eddy the Arab. He was the head bouncer. And he was actually Polish. I saw his paystub once. But he looked like something left over from the stampede scene in *Lawrence of Arabia*. Besides he carried a long curved Omar Sharifian knife in his cummerbund. Just for show, as far as I know.

I suppose all this doesn't make bartending sound all that wonderful, but it had its moments. It was a thrill, for instance, after working there for a few months to have a waiter come up to you at the service bar, slam down his tray and bark: "Two CCs one VO, a rusty nail with a lime twist and a Guinness off the shelf." And to see almost like in a movie both your hands shoot out to fill the order. I learned to pour perfect shots. With both hands. At once.

I learned to mix fairly decent margueritas and Manhattans and martinis—and to wonder why so many mixed drinks start with M. On a really good night, Gus would leave the odd Singapore sling or lady's slipper to me—but not the really tricky ones. Nope, when the order came in for an angels kiss or a pousse cafe (which are more architecturally stunning than they are pleasing to the palate) well, that was the province of Gus the Greek, who would shoulder me aside with a "Brrrringuh da Kaluah outta my way shaddapa doan boddah me."

I remember great moments in the bar. The time we just about had a full-scale brawl on our hands. A big meaty, mean-mouthed drunk kicking tables and chairs aside, wading after another guy. He should've noticed Nick—the waiter standing just off his starboard quarter. Nick settled everything by raising his steel drink tray in a great two-handed overhead arc and bringing it down on the berserker's head. Sounded like Big Ben striking one. Could always spot Nick's drink tray after that. It was the one with a skull sized mesa in the middle.

Then there was the rat. Our bar had a giant rat. Greenhorns seeing it for the first time insisted it was a small dog, but old-timers who knew better said no, it was a rat all right. Just an uncommonly large one, is all.

The rat didn't show up all that often, but when it did, it was usually a Saturday night when the place was packed. I wasn't crazy about the rat, but there was one waiter who was absolutely terrified of him. Harry. Hadn't seen the rat, you understand, but just knew he was going to, one night.

He was right. I was there when it happened. Harry was whistling across the floor with a full tray of drinks balanced on his palm, rounded a table . . . and there dead ahead, he saw two little yellow eyes in a big swatch of brown fur. Harry went into a Flintstone skid. The tray of drinks went into orbit. Harry shrieked and jumped for the highest ground he could find on short notice, wrapping his arms around a pole and clinging for dear life.

Regrettably for Harry, the Pole he wrapped his arms around was Eddy the Arab.

Ah yes. The rat. Eddy the Arab . . . Gus the Greek . . . "Gimme two CCs, a VO, one rusty nail with a lime twist and a Guinness off the shelf . . ."

Yup. Whenever I get sick of the writing business I think back to the good old days, tending bar. Makes this business seem like a piece of cake.

Bald and Proud

*Sooner or later almost every radio broadcaster must
face his personal moment of truth. Mine came at the
open house held by the CBC Radio program,* Fresh
Air, *in the spring of 1983. I had to walk out on a stage
in the Cabbagetown studio and face an auditorium full
of faithful* Fresh Air *listeners, 99 percent of whom had
never seen me before.*

Well it was really heartening to see all you folks who turned up on
a Saturday morning in Toronto, but to tell you the truth, I'm a
little bit sorry it happened.

See, working on the radio is a . . . strange . . . way to make a living. You spend most of your working hours in a goldfish bowl of
a studio with a pair of earmuffs on your head . . . talking into what
looks like an armour-clad ice cream cone.

There is no one in the room with you. You're wearing earmuffs.
You're talking to an ice cream cone.

People have done long stretches in institutions with quilted
walls wearing jackets that button up the back, for a lot less than
that.

The thing about radio is, you can talk and talk and talk into that microphone . . . but you have no real proof that anyone, anywhere is listening.

That's the unreal and slightly disconcerting side of radio, but there's another side to it. A radio broadcaster can't see his audience. But on the plus side of the ledger, the audience can't see the broadcaster.

For whole years at a time I can hide behind my microphone nattering away . . . I don't have to wear a tie . . . my socks needn't match . . . I could do the whole thing in my pyjamas. (I think New Year's Day I did do it in my pyjamas.) And no one is the wiser.

And then something like this *Fresh Air* Open House comes along and spoils everything. You're able to see me. And I don't look anything like you thought I'd look. I'm older or younger; I'm fatter or I'm shorter, seedier or frumpier than you thought I'd be.

But most of all, I'm *balder* than you thought I'd be. People just always assume that people they've never met will have a full head of hair. Don't know why. Something like 68 percent of all males experience severe erosion of the hairline long before they get their old age pension. I see a respectable pattern of unadorned pates before me in the audience. Ex-prime minister Trudeau, notwithstanding a few heroic and overworked wisps, was bald. Julius Caesar was bald. Well, perhaps I shouldn't pursue that particular line of reasoning.

No, the thing about being bald is, it's not really *good* for anything. Little boys, when they grow up, want to be cowboys or firemen or Mounties. They never plan on being bald. There's no glamour or money in it.

But it has its advantages, being bald. Less bathroom time for one thing. My father, who was balder than I am, used to comb his hair with a damp washcloth.

On the other hand, all the young athletes in the locker room at my handball court are developing hernias from the hair dryers they have to haul around. Can't go out of the locker room without fluffing and teasing and strafing their hair with long whining bursts of hot screaming air until it's as dry as a patch of Arizona scrub pine.

Needless to say, I invariably beat them to the bar.

You save more than time by being bald. I get very few certificates of appreciation from shareholders in Brylcreem, thanking me for my continued support. I don't much worry about whether my shampoo is full-bodied, extra rich, vitaminized, ultra-organic or pH balanced.

If I find small white drifts on my shoulders I know I'm in the middle of a snowstorm, not a dandruff attack.

Most of all, being bald is a tremendously liberating experience. It frees you from worry. Worry about going bald. You *are* bald. You don't have to think about it anymore, and you can take it from there.

Unfortunately, male vanity being the awesome force it is, a lot of baldies take it to their friendly neighbourhood rugmaker. They shell out several hundred dollars for a toupée or a hairpiece, and that's a big mistake, I think. Frank Sinatra wears a toupée. Burt Reynolds wears a toupée and everybody *knows* Frank Sinatra and Burt Reynolds wear toupées. So why bother?

And even if I spent thousands and got the ultimate toupée, I'm convinced that *I'd* never be convinced. I'd always worry that it was slipping over one eye, or that the colour didn't match, or the price tag was showing. In other people's eyes I'd always read that haunting Clairol refrain: "Does he or doesn't he?" Who needs it?

Hair transplants? No thanks. Anytime I'm tempted to pay for the thrill of having divots of hair yanked from my chest and slammed into my scalp I'll think about Bobby Hull. He had a hair transplant a few years ago. Had it all done in one weekend, between games. You're not supposed to have it done in one weekend. Bobby Hull came out of it with blackened eyes, a swollen nose and looking altogether like he'd been mugged by the entire first line of the Philadelphia Flyers. His eyes and nose look fine now, but the hair that grows on Bobby Hull's head looks exactly like the hair that ought to be growing on Bobby Hull's chest. When Bobby Hull comes on my TV to sell me a can of motor oil, I have the uncomfortable feeling that I'm being addressed by a man wearing alfalfa sprouts.

Naw, transplants aren't the answer. Toupées aren't the answer. So what is the answer? Well, the answer is to learn to live with it. Baldness I mean. More than that—to rejoice in it.

It's time for us skinheads to come out of the closet. Be bald and proud. We obviously have nothing to hide. We'll stop talking about lack of hair. We'll call ourselves hirsutely disadvantaged. Better than that—we won't talk of going bald, we'll talk of "gaining face." Wholesale changes! Why shouldn't this very program be re-christened "Fresh Hair"?

We shall have our pantheon of hairless heroes. Sir John A. was bald. Picasso was bald. Sir Winston . . . ah . . . Sir Winston. Do you know what Lady Astor once said to Churchill? She said: "Winston, if you were my husband I should flavour your coffee with poison."

And Churchill raised that great, grizzled, bulldog-faced, bald head of his, regarded the woman sourly for a moment and replied, "Madam, if I were your husband I should drink it."

I'd *shave* my head to get off a line like that.

Wild Excuses for Speeding

This is kind of a personal question but . . . how do you handle cops? When they pull you over, I mean. I'm not very good at it. Of course I suppose it's reasonable to feel like the cat's got your tongue when you're conversing with a steely-eyed gent who happens to have a .38 Smith and Wesson on his hip, but I'm *really* not good at it. Even when I'm not guilty of impaired driving or going through a stop sign or failing to yield or whatever I'm being pulled over for.

Once upon a time I used to have coffee with a cop in downtown Toronto. He was an easy going, young guy with a wry sense of humour and a pretty good perspective on himself and the job he was doing. I remember one morning joking about getting pulled over and he suddenly turned . . . *not* so easy going. His eyes got real hard and flat like Clint Eastwood's in a spaghetti western.

"What I hate," he said, "are all the ways you drivers try to con us." It was the way the drivers talked *down,* he said. The way they seemed to automatically assume that anybody is smart enough to outwit a dumb flatfoot. Nobody ever feels bad, he said, about lying to a cop. And when the lies don't work, they often turn to abuse and contempt and even threats.

"Every driver seems to have a brother-in-law who's the desk sergeant," mused the cop. "If I had a dollar for every driver who swore he'd have my badge lifted . . . well, I wouldn't be sitting here drinking coffee."

I wish he hadn't told me all that, the cop. I was guilty of just about everything he said, short of the brother-in-law desk sergeant.

I hadn't thought of that. But the next time I got stopped, I was twice as bad.

I've exhausted the possibilities of fake humility. "Officer, I realize you're doing your job and klutzes like me don't make it easier. I swear it won't happen again." He gives me a ticket.

I've tried fake outrage. "Now see here, Officer, you know and I know that nobody in their right mind comes to a full halt at a stop sign in the middle of the country." Ticket.

I've tried bribery. "By golly you're right that is a twenty-dollar bill folded in over my ownership." Ticket.

And I've tried fake camaraderie. "Say weren't you and your lovely wife at the policeman's ball I spoke at last spring?" Another ticket.

One time I was tootling down the highway on my way home from work . . . a few . . . miles over the speed limit, I guess. I heard the familiar banshee wail, checked the mirror and saw the old cherries popping at me. Aw boy. Nailed again. What'll I use this time?

And it came to me. In a flash. Like Saul during his commute to Damascus. No excuses this time! I will tell, by God, the truth.

I got out of the car feeling like the guy on *100 Huntley Street* looks. "Officer," I beamed, "you got me fair and square. I was speeding. I would estimate that I was doing between five and ten miles over the speed limit. You have every right to give me a ticket and I expect one." I smiled. And waited. He gave me a ticket. For doing fifty in a thirty. Plus a summons for a faulty tail light.

Which leads inevitably to a news story out of Indianapolis. A story told by speed trap operator Lee Hyland of the Marion County Sheriff's Office, Indiana. He told of stopping a speeder who went through his trap at a very high rate of speed. He confronted the driver, who said (now listen, this is good)—the driver told the cop that he had been preoccupied trying to kill a bee that was flying around his car, and that, "My foot must have pushed the gas pedal down a little too much." He even produced the dead bee.

Isn't that good? Would you have thought of that? Unfortunately Lieutenant Lee Hyland of the Marion County Sheriff's Office is nobody's fool. He asked to see the bee a little closer. The bee, he noted, had dust on its wings.

"This bee had been dead for months," says Lieutenant Hyland, "the man kept it on his dashboard in case he ever got stopped."

The driver got a ticket. Lieutenant Hyland won first prize in the "Wildest Excuse for Speeding Contest," sponsored by the Police League of Indiana. First prize: a hand-held police radar scanner. Moral: if you're driving through Marion County, Indiana, drive carefully.

And if you must speed a little, be sure to dust your bee.

That Old Black Magic

1989

Can't Lose If You Don't Buy a Ticket

I don't buy lottery tickets—and it's not because I'm a prude. Some of my best friends, etc. It's not because I'm an unreconstructed Calvinist who believes you shouldn't get something for nothing, either. Anybody who's had cause to work alongside me knows that my adherence to any Work Ethic is directly related and inversely proportional to the proximity of a shady tree and/or a tall, cool one.

No, the truth is, I don't buy lottery tickets because I'm afraid someday I might actually win. Then I'd really be up the creek.

The problem with winning a lottery is the *suddenness* of it all. One day you're a working stiff shuffling along in the bus queue, the next day you're a capitalist pig plutocrat dealing in stock portfolios with one hand while you light twenty-dollar Havana coronas with the other. I couldn't take the pressure change. My eardrums would pop, or something.

Think about it before you lay out your money for the next 649. Are you really prepared to deal with all those relatives fawning all over you—the ones who, just last week, wouldn't have spit in your ear if your brain was on fire?

And what about the cons and scams you're going to have to contend with? The hustlers and rustlers that will be tracking you down, phoning you up, filling your mailbox, and waiting to flag you down at the end of your driveway to beg you to invest, donate, loan, or underwrite? The days of strolling down to an H and R Block office with a shoebox full of crumpled receipts under your arm are gone forever, bucko. From now on, you'll need your own personal, twenty-four-hour-a-day accountant and a lawyer—no, make that a whole firm of lawyers—just to protect your interests and keep your finances in order.

While you're at it, better hire a second firm of lawyers to keep an eye on the first one.

Speaking of getting flagged down, have you considered the very real possibility of being kidnapped and held for ransom now that you've won a lottery? Could happen. And not just to you but possibly your loved ones. Might as well start looking into electronic security systems, steel mesh fencing, and barbed wire. Your cocker spaniel's going to look mighty silly waddling out to sniff fire hydrants with his own personal Doberman in tow, but that's the price you have to pay for being rich.

You've barely crept over the threshold into the world of the well-heeled and already you've got headaches galore—and we haven't even mentioned the monster migraine of the piece: friends.

You don't have any friends anymore. Oh, you'll have old pals who'll swear the money doesn't make a lick of difference, but who's kidding whom? And even if *they* believe what they're saying, do *you?* From now on you will never know whether somebody likes you because of your cute nose or that even cuter bulge in your bank balance.

Not that I speak from experience or anything. I mean, I've never won a lottery—though not for lack of trying. Years ago, when it first became chic for governments to make money the same way card-sharps and racketeers do, I used to buy a lottery ticket for a draw that was held every Thursday night. After a few months of not winning I decided to increase my chances by buying a book of tickets every Thursday night.

I noticed two things: (a) I still didn't win; (b) Friday mornings had become my least favourite time of the week. I'd become grumpy, testy, and out of sorts. Sometimes the mood would slop right over Friday evening and ruin my weekend.

I finally analysed the problem. I was suffering from Greed Hangover. I'd spent much of the week fantasizing about what was going to happen when I won the Thursday night lottery. Come Friday morning I was still in debt, still nosing the same old grindstone. And I resented it.

I told my problem to a gambler I know. He's a guy who makes his living, such as it is, off the ponies, football, hockey and boxing. He laughed in my face. "You buy lottery tickets?" he sneered. "Biggest sucker bet in the world. Better you should bet the Canucks or the Leafs than lotteries. Statistical fact: ya got more chance o' bein' hit by lightning than ya have o' winnin' a lottery."

That did it for me—the lightning statistic. Haven't bought a lottery ticket since.

Right now, everybody in the office is going nuts about the big lottery coming up this week. They'll be sitting there on the night of the draw, dreaming big dreams, clutching their crumpled stubs in sweaty palms.

Not me. I plan to take a nice long walk while the draw takes place.

Mind you, if I get struck by lightning, I'm going to be really browned off.

Where Was I?

All right. I accept that I have this . . . disease . . . condition . . . affliction—whatever you want to call it. I can live with that. After all, I'm in good company. The great writer G.K. Chesterton suffered from it. So did Tennyson and Toscanini and Albert Einstein and just about every writer and/or academic I've ever met. Heck, there's even a whole subgenre of jokes about academics who have it.

You know . . . the Absent-minded Professor jokes.

Well, I didn't get the letters after my name, but I definitely got the adjectives in front. I'm absent-minded. I forget . . . a lot. And not just the little things like putting the cat out and whether I have anything at the cleaners and what oil I run in my car in the summer—I forget the big things, too. Things like dinner invitations. The name of the boss's wife. The location of Mutual Street. I work on Mutual Street. Telephone numbers? Everybody forgets telephone numbers. I forget *my* telephone number.

Here—honestly—is how one morning went for me two weeks ago: wake up half-hour late (forgot to set alarm), slam through usual predawn rituals of shave, shower, and rooting for matching socks while juggling mug of tepid Nescafé. Out of house and into car. Out of car and back to house for car keys. Back to car. Back to house while car warming up to make sure kettle turned off. Back to car to wrench keys out of ignition because house key on same key ring. Kettle is, of course, off. Back to car. On road at last, but only for two miles at which point execute desperate U-turn and return to house. Reason: cannot remember if I shut garage door. Had. Leave driveway once again in squeal of tires and sulphurous cloud of undeleted expletives that would have brought a blush to blue-black jowls of Richard Nixon himself. Decide to count blessings: at least there's not much traffic. Small detonation in nether reaches of consciousness—*why* not much traffic this morning? Check Timex digital on left wrist and divine answer. There is not much traffic this morning because it's Saturday morning. Most people don't go to work on Saturday mornings.

Including me.

Absent-mindedness—what a wonderfully evocative term. The mind is AWOL. Not in. Where does it go? You'd think if God was such a hot engineer, he might have turned us out with foreheads like illuminated dashboards that could light up during bouts of absent-mindedness. Just a short answering-machine-style message to avoid embarrassment and misunderstanding: "Hi! Arthur's mind's not in right now, but your call is important to him. Please try again later."

I wonder if we aren't all more forgetful these days. Bet we are. Look at the caveman—what did he have to remember? Come in out of the rain; keep your fingers out of the flames; if it's smaller than you, bash it over the head and eat it; if it's bigger than you, run like hell— that was pretty well it. Even in my grandfather's time there were not what you'd call serious overdrafts on the average memory bank. Back then a fella could get by just by remembering when to say gee! and when to say haw!; how to tell when the wheat was ripe and how long it took to drive thirty head of cattle from the barnyard to the abat- toir. That and a couple of verses of "The Old Rugged Cross" would probably get you through. My grandfather did not have to bother his head remembering his social insurance number. Nor did my grand- dad have to remember a fifteen-digit driver's licence, eight numbers on a medical insurance card, another eight for a personal chequing account, and the combination of the lock on a ten-speed.

Maybe that's why my mind seems to be more absent than usual. Maybe my mental floppy disc is full.

Which is another example of how modern life gives us more, not less, to remember. Before I could write this piece I had to remember to turn on my keyboard, turn on my monitor, then insert two floppy discs in my computer. I had to remember that one of them is called MS-DOS and the other is called MS-WORD VERSION 3.1. When I started out in the writing business twenty years ago, all I had to remember was the capital W on my Olivetti was broken and to change the ribbon every six months or so.

But it's not just computers, it's everything—parking, even. Have you seen the parking lot at Canada's Wonderland? It's bigger than most of the Benelux countries! I will never go to Canada's Wonderland because I know the gods are just daring me to park in that tract and then try to find my car at the end of the day.

I take it back. I may pay a visit, but I'll go by cab.

I have an abiding mistrust of parking lots, and so, I imagine, does James Hawk. Mr. Hawk is a prominent lawyer who practises in Portsmouth, Virginia. One evening Mr. Hawk skipped out of his office at close of day and down to his customary parking space, only to find it empty. His shiny new Cougar two-door was gone. Hawk called the police, then his insurance company. The police got right on the case while the insurance company hustled a rental car over for Hawk to use. The next day our lawyer arrived at work in his rental car, only to find that someone else had beaten him to his usual parking space. So he drove to a nearby city parking lot and pulled in.

Right beside his missing Cougar.

Which is when it all came back to Mr. Hawk—how two days ago, finding his favourite parking spot occupied, he had parked his own car in the municipal lot—right where it still, in fact, was.

Mind you, Annie McDonnell of Larchmont, New York, got an even stiffer jolt. She was fixing herself a late breakfast one morning when the doorbell rang. She opened the door to find her husband, Jim, standing there. "Hello, Anne," he said.

An unremarkable enough exchange—except for the fact that Mrs. McD. had not laid eyes on Mr. McD. for fifteen years—not since he'd suddenly disappeared after bumping his head in a fall. Jim McDonnell had spent the missing decade and a half working as a short-order cook and bartender in Philadelphia and answering to the name of Jim Peters. Finally something jogged his memory. Jim

Peters of Philadelphia recalled that he was really Jim McDonnell of Larchmont. He caught the next train home.

Those stories both feature the three scariest things I know about absent-mindedness: it's easy; it's involuntary; and worst of all, the ramifications are impossible to foretell. Today, you might forget where you put your sunglasses; tomorrow, you could be grilling cheese dogs in Philadelphia.

There is, of course, one explanation of my affliction that I've avoided mentioning—the notion that perhaps there's nothing wrong with me at all. Or rather, nothing more than the normal wear and tear one would expect to find in a mileage-heavy machine that's been flicked on and off for forty-four years and expected to make sense of grocery lists, the east-west subway line, the Blue Jays' bull-pen, the formula for finding the circumference of a circle . . . and where I left the car keys.

Maybe there's nothing wrong with my mind at all. Maybe I'm just getting . . . you know . . .

Old?

Well, if I am, I hope I learn to handle absent-mindedness with the aplomb of Alfred Edward Matthews. Mr. Matthews was a character actor who first appeared on stage in 1886. He was still going strong right up until his death in 1960.

Well, *strong* may be too precise a word. Mr. Matthews could still deliver a stirring performance, but once past his seventieth birthday he found himself blowing the odd line here and there.

Such as the time, deep in the sunset of his career, when he appeared in a West End play. His part required him to cross the stage and answer a crucial telephone call.

The phone rang. Mr. Matthews strode across stage, picked up the receiver . . .

And completely forgot who he was supposed to be talking to or what he was expected to say.

Alfred Edward Matthews may have suffered from absent-mindedness, but his talent for improvisation was well oiled. Holding out the telephone receiver to the only other actor on the stage, Matthews thundered imperiously:

"It's for you!"

Our Symbol—The Rat

I believe I have discovered the very headwaters whence springeth Canada's renowned reputation for meekness and compliance beneath and below the norm. It's our national mascot, the beaver. If Canada wants to play hardball with the big guys, then the buck-toothed rodent with the bug eyes has got to go.

That revelation struck me while browsing through a book entitled *The Bestiary: A Book of Beasts, Being a Translation from the Latin Bestiary of the Twelfth Century.* That's where I came across the following:

> This is an animal called the *Beaver,* none more gentle, and his testicles make a capital medicine. For this reason . . . when he notices that he is being pursued by the hunter, he removes his own testicles with a bite, and casts them before the sportsman, and thus escapes by flight. What is more, if he should again happen to be chased by a second hunter, he lifts himself up and shows his members to him, and the latter, when he perceives the testicles to be missing, leaves the Beaver alone . . . The creature is called a Beaver (Castor) because of the castration.

It is difficult to guess just which nonprescription chemicals the twelfth-century reporter who recorded those observations might have been ingesting. Beavers, of course, do no such thing. They couldn't if they wanted to, as their testicles are internal. And yet the name—Castor—and the image—wimpy—endure.

Well, doesn't the foregoing sound like a fair metaphorical reprise for the faltering diffidence our country displays on the international stage? Bush denounces, Thatcher chastizes, other nations preen and strut and posture . . . and here comes Bucky the Honest Broker, hiking up his guard hairs, exclaiming in a shrill falsetto, "See? No threat here! We're harmless! Don't mind us, folks, we're just here to check the waterworks!"

It's ironic that Canadians, who have been fighting the stereotype of being hewers of wood and drawers of water, should select as their symbol the original hewer of wood and, well, dammer of water. America has the majestic eagle, the Soviet Union the mighty bear. Great Britain gives equal time to ferocious lions and stubborn bulldogs; Frenchmen line up behind a comely and capable-looking Amazon called Liberty . . .

We chose a rat.

A healthy rat, I grant you. A clean-living, outdoorsy, industrious, and unusually clean rat—but a rat for all that.

And not a terribly bright one, either. Before the rapaciousness of the European fur traders decimated their numbers, beavers were so plentiful and docile that Indians knocked them off with sticks. After three centuries of hot pursuit, the beaver is only marginally more prudent, still easy prey for pelt hunters with a single-shot .22 or the most rudimentary of traps.

Back in the 1700s a North American Indian with a finely honed sense of drollery remarked to a Jesuit priest, "The beaver does everything perfectly well; it makes kettles, hatchets, swords, knives, bread; and in short it makes everything."

In short, the Indian was absolutely right; Europeans paid well for the beaver. In the long term, it was quite a different story. The traders brought dazzling luxuries and captivating trinkets the likes of which the Indians had never known. Mind you, they'd never known smallpox, typhus, venereal disease, alcoholism, or lust for money, either. They got those, too.

Perhaps the most sinister stowaway that sneaked from the *canots du nord* into the Indian encampments was an abstract one: total dependence on a single, fragile industry. In the early years of the nineteenth century an Indian chief saw it all coming and laid it out for explorer David Thompson: "We are now killing the beaver without any labor," he said. "We are now rich, but shall soon be poor, for when the Beaver are destroyed we have nothing to depend on to purchase what we want for our families. Strangers now overrun our country with their iron traps, and we, and they will soon be poor."

That was about the size of it. In the early 1800s the fur trade collapsed as precipitously as it had begun. The furs were suddenly too far inland and too sparse to chase. Relations were dodgy among the superpowers of the day—England, France, and those belligerent Yankee upstarts to the south. And anyway, Europe didn't seem all that interested in beaver hats anymore. Some enterprising haberdasher had come up with a technique of lacquering silk and turning it into headgear that was lighter, cheaper, and almost instantly *à la mode*.

Many fortunes were made during the fur trade—none of them by the Indians who were the very spine of it. In the waning years of the enterprise, a Saulteaux chief by the name of Peguis looked around and lamented:

"Before you whites came to trouble the ground, our rivers were full of fish and woods of deer. Our creeks abounded with beavers and our plains were covered with buffaloes. But now we are brought to poverty. Our beaver are gone forever . . ."

Well, not quite, Peguis. It certainly looked as if things would wind up that way as the beaver waddled to the edge of extinction. But we all overlooked that one activity the beaver practises even more diligently than dam building. It's a phenomenon to which human eyes are not privy, going on, as it does, behind the impermeable walls of the beaver lodge. The mechanics of the operation are the beavers' secret; all we know is that, whatever the beavers do in there, it results in an awful lot of little beavers. The animal is so prolific that despite continued trapping, encroaching suburbs, intruding highways, shrinking wetlands, air pollution, water degradation, acid rain, the question of Palestinian autonomy—despite all the Bad

Things that seem to mitigate against all that is good and true these days—the beaver is flourishing.

Better than that—what used to be our endangered species of indigenous dam builders has become . . . well, just a damned nuisance, actually. In Saskatchewan the beavers are creating such agricultural havoc that the provincial government recently launched a Nuisance Beaver Program to prune the rodents' furry ranks.

Government sanction to kill the National Symbol? Isn't that . . . un-Canadian, sorta?

Don't ask me—ask Argentina. Preferably on a clean, well-lit street among plenty of reliable witnesses.

Argentinians know all about our national emblem. Back in 1946 the Canadian government gave that country twenty-five pairs of the critters as a gesture of international goodwill. I don't know the Spanish for "Go forth and multiply," but the beavers must have figured it out pretty quickly. When their travelling cages were opened they took one look around, saw a land full of gnaw-able timber, dam-able rivers, and Glory be, not a natural predator in sight . . . and they went to work. And play. In the next forty years Canada's furry foreign aid chalked up an Argentine rap sheet that included everything from chewing down the country's softwood forests to flooding valuable sheep pastures to disrupting the spawning patterns of trout.

The beavers also obviously did a lot of cuddling on those nippy Argentine nights. Authorities there would dearly love to gather up Canada's gift and pop it in the mail in a plain brown carton marked Return to Sender. Trouble is, the original twenty-five beavers have swollen to an estimated *25,000.*

Beavers. I know (only casually) a pair that live in a pond about five minutes walk from my back door. Every once in a while when the world gets too much with me, I wander over there and sit on a log to watch them doing their yardwork. They ignore me, just as they ignore the busy highway nearby, the kids noisily hunting frogs, and the Air Canada 747 from Winnipeg that drones overhead each afternoon about 3:30.

My beavers couldn't care less. They just go on shuttling across their custom-made pond, catering to the Unseen Foreman as they have for centuries—millennia perhaps. Living. Thriving. Not terrorizing or subjugating or proselytizing or taunting or threatening or humiliating or patronizing their neighbours. Just doing what they do as well as they can do it.

Not a bad lifestyle . . . for a rat.

Not a bad example for a country, either.

Boys and Dogs

A boy can learn a lot from a dog: obedience, loyalty, and the importance of turning around three times before lying down.

—ROBERT BENCHLEY

Without becoming overly sober-sided on the subject, I'd like to point out that a boy can learn a whole lot more than that from dogs. I speak if not as an authority then at least as a veteran who has at one time or another pampered and paper trained, coaxed and cursed, romped with and stumbled over five or six in-house mutts. Some of them were better than others, but I remember even the most forgettable of them with infinitely greater clarity than, say, anybody in my Grade 10 class.

The first dog in my life was Willy, short for Wilhelmina. As with most dogs, Willy came to me in a casual and unpremeditated way. She was a white-and-black vaguely fox-terrierish pup that waddled out of the folds of my sister's raincoat and onto our kitchen linoleum one evening when I was still a preschooler. Willy had been kidnapped. My sister had rescued her from a revolving restaurant stool. Her drunken owner kept trying to set Willy on the stool and Willy, not surprisingly, kept falling off. After the third swan dive, my sister pounced. She scooped up the pup, tongue-lashed the drunk, and swept out the door and down the street before he had time to hiccup.

Willy was a squat and stumpy pooch that grew to become . . . well, squatter and stumpier, actually. There wasn't much that was remarkable about Willy, aside from her predilection for walking on three legs as opposed to four. Whenever she got going at a pretty good clip, Willy would just tuck a rear leg—sometimes the left, sometimes the right—up close to her belly and chug along on the other three. She wasn't favouring an injury and she didn't limp. In fact, you wouldn't even know about the reserve limb unless you actually counted the paws that were hitting the ground. Willy on three legs could stay ahead of the four-legged competition, even when she was in heat.

Except once. Some anonymous canine Lothario had his way with Willy on at least one occasion. The result was a litter of six puppies, one of which died at birth, four of which went to other homes, and the last of which stayed home with Momma. And me. My older sisters were moving on to more mature pastimes—notably boys. Consequently the pup was pretty well exclusively mine. I chose him mostly because of the sooty patch of hair that surrounded his right eye. I dubbed him Shiner, of course. I was eight or nine years old, and the name struck me as the very acme of wit.

For many years we did all the things that kids and dogs growing up together do—things involving rabbits and sticks and tennis balls and mock battles on the grass. I still remember the terrible day Shiner reappeared after a three-day absence.

He staggered stiff-legged across the lawn. He was hideously emaciated and his eyes were full of pain and focussed off somewhere that I couldn't see. I kept stroking his head and offering him water that he couldn't drink until he died later that evening. Distemper.

There were community dogs, too—ones that I didn't own but spent more time with than their owners did. I remember a German shepherd named Rocky. He was the Cary Grant of dogdom—the kind of dog that gives German shepherds a good name. Rocky was bright and alert. His nose was wet and his ears stood up and he had those big chestnut-coloured eyes you could practically curl up in.

He also had a butler complex. Rocky would approach visitors at the end of the driveway and escort them up to the front door by gently taking their wrist in his massive maw. A bone china teacup would have been safe in that mouth, but first-time visitors, looking down at one hundred-odd pounds of magnificently conditioned police dog, weren't always aware of that. I still remember babysitting for Rocky's folks one night and opening the front door to find Rocky on the porch with a strange man in tow. The man was sweating heavily. He was also on his knees. "Dog!" he managed to gasp out, and then, "Arm!" Over a calming pot of tea, he explained that he was a real estate agent and had been checking house numbers from the end of the driveway when he'd suddenly experienced a . . . constricting sensation between his right forearm and his briefcase. It was only Rocky, trying to be helpful.

The real estate agent panicked and started to trot toward the porch light. Rocky deduced that his guest wanted to go faster, so he picked up the pace. Trot became canter, canter became gallop. It's a cruel thought, but I have often wished I'd been able to videotape the last few yards of that incredible journey. I can visualize the real estate agent, fedora gone, overcoat flaring out behind him, briefcase bouncing through the gravel as he lurched along in a kind of desperate running half crouch, his arm clamped in the mouth of a huge dog that thought this was a wonderful game.

Rocky had a kennel colleague named Mike, also a German shepherd, but as different from Rocky as a rink rat is from Wayne Gretzky. Mike always reminded me of one of those B-movie characters played by Sal Mineo—tough kid from the slums who scrabbles through life with a chip on his shoulder and Don't Tread on Me tattooed on his forearm. Mike was one of those there-but-for-the-grace-of-God dogs. Where Rocky's coat was smooth and lustrous, Mike's was dull and kind of kinky along the spine. Rocky had eyes that made you want to sit down and tell him your troubles. Mike's eyes were furtive and shifty. Mike was the kind of dog that you instinctively walked around in a wide semicircle, with your hands in your pockets. I liked Mike, but I didn't entirely trust him.

There were other dogs in my life. I remember a dippy Dalmatian named Duchess who had one blue eye and one brown eye and not a lot of grey matter behind either of them. There was a pseudo-Labrador named Chris that I inherited in midlife (hers). Chris was mortally terrified of anything that could conceivably be mistaken for a rifle. This included yardsticks, fishing rods, garden rakes, snow shovels, French bread—anything that was long and thin and carried by humans. One look and Chris would hurl herself under the verandah where she would stay, whimpering for hours. I always regretted that I couldn't find a Freudian vet for Chris.

Ah, but then there was Angus.

I found him in a Cabbagetown pet store in the spring of 1973, just hours away from a one-way trip to the Humane Society. Instead he got to ride out of the store in my coat pocket. What came into my life as an animated dustball grew to become a full-fledged sheep dog. We called him Angus because of his obvious lineage, a certain Celtic canniness in his expression plus the fact that I purchased him for a bottle of Cutty Sark. We spent the first two years of his life together in Southern Ontario and the next decade in Thunder Bay.

Magical wouldn't be too strong a word to describe Angus. Total strangers would smile at the sight of him and come up to pat him on the head. It was reciprocal. Angus had uncritical tolerance for the entire human race. He loved everybody on sight. He was totally untrainable, but it didn't matter because aside from shedding a few bales of hair each spring, he never did anything objectionable.

Unless you happened to believe strongly in obedience and dog tricks. Angus did not deign to chase balls or fetch sticks. If commanded to Sit Up or Beg or Heel or Roll Over, he would look at you with large molten chocolate eyes that seemed to say, "Surely you don't mean me?" Then he would discreetly look away, pretending your descent into bad taste never happened.

I never figured out what Angus thought cats and rabbits and wild birds were—oddly built children, I suspect. All I know is, he might sniff them or nudge them with his nose or even put his head down between his front paws with his bum in the air, tail swishing like a feathery metronome, but he would never chase them. Bad form.

As for guard dog duties, Angus only barked at family members. To strangers, he was Mother Teresa. I have the eyewitness account of a next door neighbour who swears she saw Angus licking the hands and faces of a gang of late-night thieves trying to steal a tent from my backyard.

Angus was a flop as a hunting dog and a failure as a watchdog. He was also, paws down, the finest four-footed friend I ever had. Last summer as we prepared to move from Thunder Bay back to Southern Ontario, I worried about how a twelve-year-old dog would handle the arduous two-day car trip.

It turned out not to be a problem. Angus died in his favourite armchair on the front porch two days before the moving vans came.

E.B. White, the great American essayist, once wrote, "I can still see my first dog in all the moods and situations that memory has filed him away in. For six years he met me at the same place after school and convoyed me home—a service he thought up himself. A boy doesn't forget that sort of association."

Indeed he doesn't—no matter how old the boy might be. We have a new house now and a new dog to go with it. His name is Rufus, and the pet store he came from insists he's an Australian shepherd. He doesn't look much like an Australian shepherd. He looks like a cross between a border collie and a dingo, but that's all right. He has a good spirit and boundless energy and a pair of absurd ears that seem to rotate independently like radar dishes. He is still a chuckle-headed puppy who digs in flowerbeds, gnaws on table legs, gets swatted routinely by the family cat for his impertinence, and carries off anything he can fit in his mouth. But he's growing up. This week his voice is changing from puppy whimpers to a surprisingly deep-chested bay, the sound of which frightens him more than whatever it is he imagines he sees or hears out there. Rufus has bonded, as well. He looks to the adults of the household to feed him and let him in and out and make sure the water bowl is topped up, but his heart incontestably belongs to a young male resident by the name of Danny.

A boy and his dog. It's a corny, overworked theme, but it happens. It's happening right now, as I type this. I can see Rufus on the lawn, looking toward the front gate. His right ear is cocked, the left sits crumpled at half mast. From the way his head lists eastward I know that he's listening for the growl of the school bus as it rounds the last bend before our place. In a moment he'll start emitting little yips and his tail will thump and he'll *boing* down the lawn like a springbok to greet his master.

A boy and his dog. If Dan's life unfolds like most boys' lives, Rufus will be only the first of several canine chums.

But in countless small and immeasurable ways, he'll always be the best.

Old Prickly

Among the porcupines, rape is unknown.

A Canadian writer by the name of Greg Clark made that observation at least half a century ago. It marks one of the very few times anyone's bothered to even notice the humble porky, much less enshrine him in print.

Not the only time, though. Thumb through your copy of *Hamlet* until you find the part where the melancholy Dane gets chatted up by the ghost:

> . . . could a tale unfold whose lightest word
> Would harrow up thy soul, freeze thy young blood,
> Make thy two eyes, like stars, start from their spheres,
> Thy knotted and combined locks to part
> And each particular hair to stand on end,
> Like quills upon the fretful porpentine.

Porpentine. How typical of the porcupine's Sad Sack run of luck that in his one shot at literary immortality, Shakespeare spells his name wrong.

I always felt sorry for porcupines. They are the gentlest of creatures and, it must be said, one of the dumbest. Nature gave them neither brain nor brawn nor fang nor claw. Their eyesight is pathetic, their speed a joke. All they have to defend themselves against predators are quills, needle sharp and barbed.

Approximately 36,000 per porcupine.

It must work out pretty well because there are plenty of porcupines around. I'm told that the smarter coyotes, fishers and wolverines have learned to flip porcupines over, exposing the soft underbelly, but most of the animals that try messing with porcupines aren't that creative. The last three dogs I've owned, for instance. They all wound up with quills in their paws and their snouts—and a decided aversion to bothering porcupines ever again.

Quills serve the porcupine pretty well against his natural enemies, but they are not infallible. Each time I drive to the city I pass two, three, sometimes half a dozen prickly grey-black mounds on the pavement. Porcupines that couldn't shuffle across the road fast enough to avoid being kayoed by cars or trucks.

Against a speeding Dunlop radial, quills aren't worth a damn.

Funny animal, the porcupine. An old Finnish bushworker I knew up in Thunder Bay used to call them "the greenhorn's friend." He explained that porcupines had kept many a lost hunter or prospector from starving to death. He said that even a greenhorn with a broken leg could probably knock a porcupine out of a tree, kill it with a stick, and get some meat in his belly.

Well, the porcupine may be the greenhorn's friend but he's not exactly buddy-buddy with a lot of camp and cottage owners I know. That's because of the porkies' addiction to anything salty.

And I mean anything. If a human hand has touched it, that's like chip dip for the porcupine. They'll gnaw their way through shovel handles, paddles, canoe gunwhales, outhouse doors—you name it, the porcupine will take a chunk out of it. He's got the tools for the job: four chisel-like incisors backed up by a set of sixteen ridged cheek teeth that can grind down just about anything the incisors bite off.

For all the damage a porcupine can do, you seldom hear people cursing them the way they curse wolves and rats and groundhogs. I wonder why that is? Maybe it's because we all feel a little bit sorry for the porcupine. He is so awkward, so clumsy, so slow, and so flat-out dim-witted.

Perhaps he reminds us of the closet nerd that lives in all of us.

The poor hapless porcupine even makes a hash of romance. Peacocks and ruffed grouse strut and perform dances for their mating rituals. Moose trumpet. Deer and mountain goats have skull-bashing gladitorial contests. Even humans lay on candlelight, wine, and a little Debussy on the stereo.

What does the porcupine do?

Well, part of the mating ritual of the porcupine involves the male drenching his would-be life mate with urine.

Is this to make her, in some perversely porcupine way, more attractive to him? No. Biologists figure the point of the golden shower is to deter any other possible suitors.

Figures.

Let me leave you with the only porcupine riddle I know. It's not magnificent as riddles go, but hey, we're talking porcupines here, remember?

Question: How do porcupines make love?

Answer: Verrrrrrrrrry carefully.

Arthur! Arthur!

1991

Canada Beneath the Blankets

There's good news and there's bad news today. The bad news is that pollsters are back in the news; the good news is the pollsters have nothing to do with statistical assessments of your local town council, the provincial legislature or Parliament Hill. The pollsters in the news are not polling about politics . . . they're polling about love. Canadian style.

I dunno if it's coincidence or the impending visit of Saint Valentine and all the loopy midwinter goofiness that day inspires, but for some reason the soothsayers at Gallup and the entrail readers at Decima Research have been poring over the phenomenon of love and romance as they're practised in the Great White North, and they've stumbled across some pretty interesting findings.

According to Decima, Newfoundland wins the red garter for most amorous province in Confederation. Seventy-seven per cent of Newfoundlanders enthusiastically rate themselves as "sexually active." That's nearly 10 percent above the national average.

But what's this? Here's some exhausted Gallup pollsters weighing in with results from the West Coast. BC is where the action is, says Gallup. According to their surveys, 93 percent of British Columbians over the age of eighteen have been around the bases, compared with a paltry 81 percent of Maritimers. A Gallup vice-president went so far as to dub British Columbia "The Babylon of Canada."

Well, 93 percent in the West, 81 percent in the East . . . Ganges or Gander, Kitimat or Carbonear, the oversexed headboard and footboard of this country seem to be in fine fettle. What I want to know is, what about the rest of us in the middle? You prairie farmers. The wheat's all in . . . you got time on your hands . . . And you, Ontario—c'mon, there's more to life than making money. Quebec. Quebec? You awake?

But then Love Canadian Style has always been a bewildering business at best. A few years ago one of this country's most famous satyrs, Irving Layton, wondered why it was that a stuffy Frigidaire of a country like Canada could turn out some of the best love poetry in the world.

Layton concluded it was because, as he put it, "Canadians are a backward folk; they have not yet heard that love is dead." Adventurous folk, too. John Kenneth Galbraith, the world-famous economist and pundit, recalls his teenage years in Southwestern Ontario lust thusly:

> In winter, a cutter lent itself to lovemaking only at the cost of extreme contortion and an occasional chilling exposure. The alternative was a snowbank. Things were not appreciably more agreeable in the autumn on the frozen ground, in the spring in the mud, or in summer under the onslaught of the mosquitoes. Chastity was everywhere protected by a vigilant nature.

Vigilant, but not unbreachable. Pierre Berton defined a Canadian as someone who knows how to make love in a canoe. That's what it takes to be a citizen in a country of great lovers, I guess—a certain backwardness, a sense of adventure and above all resourcefulness. Nobody puts it more pithily than Marie Lynne Hammond who sings, "Canadian love, Canadian love . . . it's forty below or it's ninety above."

Won't be ninety above for a while yet, so stay warm, folks. And don't get distracted by a knock on the door. It's probably just a nosy pollster.

The Rolls-Royce of Pocket Knives

In that classic movie *The Third Man,* there's a scene where Orson Welles delivers the ultimate free enterprise speech. It goes: "In Italy, for thirty years under the Borgias, they had warfare, terror, murder and bloodshed, but they produced Michelangelo, Leonardo da Vinci and the Renaissance. In Switzerland, they had brotherly love, they had 500 years of democracy and peace—and what did they produce? The cuckoo clock."

Poor old Switzerland. Take away the picture postcard mountains and what have you got? Toronto. The Swiss have long been perceived as bland, boring and monotonous—and unfairly so, I think.

After all, was it not the Swiss who gave us that magic talisman lusted after by every North American male from sprout-size cub scout to aging yuppie?

I refer, of course, to the Swiss Army knife. A utensil that stands out among common pocket knives as a Rolls-Royce Silver Ghost would stand out in a fleet of Checker cabs.

The Swiss Army knife is the red one with the white cross emblazoned on its flank. But that's just the outside of the knife—it's the innards that separate the Swiss Army from all the other buck, barlow, pen, jack and clasp knives.

Packing a Swiss Army knife is like carrying a toolbox in your hip pocket. Even the simplest model gives you a nail file, tweezers, scissors and a toothpick along with the knife blade. But if you really want to get into it, you can order the SwissChamp—which has twenty-nine "blades"—or, for terminal gadget freaks, the SOS model, which boasts forty fold-out features including a ball-point pen, a fish scaler, a wood saw and a magnifying glass.

Apparently a lot of North Americans do want to get into it. Last year we bought more than $25 million worth of the little red gizmos.

The Swiss have been making the knives for nearly a hundred years, but the first time they showed up in North America was in the kitbags of Canadian and American soldiers returning from Europe after World War II. Hungry for European souvenirs, our guys had bought or swapped for them with Swiss soldiers. Since everybody in the Swiss Army seemed to carry one, our soldiers dubbed them "Swiss Army knives." The name stuck.

The North American love affair with the Swiss import shows no signs of abating. Victorinox Cutlery of Switzerland now pumps out sixty different models of the Swiss Army knife and the US market alone sucks up 35 percent of them.

The question is why? Why are all we soft-palmed, pudgy-bellied, by-and-large urban guys buying a tool that theoretically only Robinson Crusoe could need?

Be honest—when's the last time you grabbed your pocket knife to scale a lake trout, strip an electrical wire or to read the fine print in your mortgage?

Have you ever actually tried to *use* the wood-saw blade in a Swiss Army knife? I have. Yesterday, as an experiment, I decided to "fell" a poplar about five inches in diameter out behind my place, using only my knife.

I did it, but it took a long time and left me with two blisters on my palm. I think I could've managed it a little faster if I'd just used my teeth.

So why do we keep buying them? Because we're romantics. There is a segment of the Canadian male populace, the members of which are Truly Handy. They can set the timing on their lawnmowers, find studs in the wall, mix cement, put up wallpaper and barbecue a steak to perfection. There are precisely thirty-seven such Canadian males and they wouldn't think of buying a Swiss Army knife.

The rest of us are technological nerds. Woody Allen is our patron saint. We can barely change a lightbulb or remember which key goes in the ignition. We buy the Swiss Army knives because we think they give us an edge.

They don't, of course. What they give is a huge belly laugh to those thirty-seven Truly Handy guys. They also provide a tidy income to the Swiss gnomes who keep selling them to us.

Ah, the Swiss: they may be bland and monotonous—but they ain't stupid.

It's a Girl! (Father Expected to Live)

I have before me a report in the *Canadian Journal of Anaesthesia* suggesting that fathers should think twice before venturing into the delivery room to get "personally involved" in the birth of their children.

I have several responses to a proposal such as that—two of which are: "No kidding," and "*Now* they tell me."

Where were these experts when I needed them—in the delivery room of St. Joseph's Hospital when my daughter was being born? This, of course, was several years ago. Back in the Age of Mariposa and Woodstock—a Caring, Sharing, Involved and Happening Era when friends in bandanas and denim would say, "Naturally you'll be attending the birth with your wife." "Yup," you would reply. "Oh, sure. You bet. Wouldn't have it any other way."

But of *course* you would share the sacred birth process. Wasn't that what Life Was All About?

Well, yes. Yes, it is. But, friends . . .

It's messy.

It's more than messy—it's mortifying.

Thoreau once said: "Beware of any enterprise that requires new clothes." Black's Corollary reads: "Be extra leery of any enterprise that requires paper slippers and a surgical mask." That's what they dress maternity room Dad voyeurs in—paper slippers and a surgical mask. Then they ask you if you'd mind if a class of student nurses watches the birth.

Now think about this: you are in a room with your wife who is naked and in some considerable distress. The two of you are poised uneasily on the cusp of one of the biggest days of your life. The authorities want to know if you'd mind if a herd of strangers takes notes. If it happened in your living room, at your office, on the street—anywhere that was even close to your own turf, you would tell the authorities to go pound Sifto, but you are in a strange room full of sundry stainless steel mysteries not to mention tubes and dials and you are wearing paper slippers and a surgical mask. Cowlike, you nod your assent.

Cheer up—this is only the first assault on your dignity. Soon the doctor comes. You can tell he's the doctor because the maternity room staff defers to him. Besides, he's got the rubber gloves on and his surgical mask is regular-issue cloth, not cheap paper like yours.

It's good that you have these clues to the doctor's identity because you'd never figure out who he was from his conversation. He talks like your garage mechanic. He chats about the weather and the Blue Jays and his golf game. He offers his analysis of the current stock market slump. He crows about the gas mileage he gets with his BMW.

And as he talks, this doctor this *stranger!*—is doing unspeakable things with his hands to your soulmate. But casually! Offhandedly, as it were, like a butcher rearranging the cold cuts in his display cooler.

This is an outrage! A flagrant flouting of everything you hold dear! Are you just gonna stand there like a schnook and allow this to go on? Aren't you going to roar like a bull, rage like a tiger and put these interlopers in their place with your icy, rapier wit?

Wearing paper slippers and a surgical mask? Get serious.

In any case, it will soon get worse. The birthing process is moving along briskly. Your wife is howling and panting and perspiring, pausing only briefly to denounce you, at the top of her lungs, as the source of all pain and evil in the world. You ask her to remember the breathing exercises. She asks you to perform something that is both dexterously demanding and impossible to repeat in a gentle, family-oriented volume such as this.

And now the doctor is brandishing a . . . what is that thing, anyway? A fencing sword? A jackhammer? A jousting lance? No. It is a needle. And he is going to give it to your wife. Oh, my God!!!

That's all I remember. They tell me I hit my head quite a clip on the stirrup on my way to the floor.

Did I mention that we had a beautiful baby girl? My wife told me all about it in the recovery room. Mine, not hers.

What's a Clerihew, Anyhew?

I've been thinking about four men who gave their names to the world of humour. They are: Mr. Thomas Swift, the Reverend Spooner, Edmund Bentley and Claude Emile Jean-Baptiste Litre.

The first two are the best known. Mr. Swift gave us the famous "Tom Swiftie" jokes, as in: "Hmmm, sun's going down," said Tom darkly.

And "Am I ever getting fat," declared Tom roundly.

Also my favourite: "Why, that chicken has no beak," the man pronounced impeccably.

Those are all Tom Swifties.

He explained rapidly.

Spoonerisms, on the other hand, are rather more complicated. They owe their existence to the Reverend William Archibald Spooner, a turn-of-the-century Oxford dean who had the unfortunate habit of transposing letters in the words he spoke. Often very critical letters.

Thus, a toast from the lips of the Reverend to dear old Queen Victoria came out, "Let us drink to the queer old dean."

And who can forget the famous Spooner sermon that contained the phrase: "Ah, but our Lord is a shoving leopard."

Edmund Bentley was another old Englishman with an equally odd perspective on the English tongue. He liked to write little poems about famous people. People like Voltaire. Of him, Bentley wrote:

It was a weakness of Voltaire's
To forget to say his prayers
And which, to his shame
He never overcame.

What to call these fey little quatrains invented by Edmund Bentley? Edmunds? Bentleys? No. Edmund is too common and a Bentley is a car. Fortunately Edmund Bentley had a middle name that fits the bill perfectly. Which is why we call his comic inventions "clerihews."

And that brings us to the fourth man I mentioned: Claude Emile Jean-Baptiste Litre.

Monsieur Litre was an eighteenth-century maker of wine bottles and the father of the metric litre—facts that were largely lost in history until they were recently made public by researchers at the University of Waterloo, Ontario. Well, it's not often that major figures of science are forgotten, then rediscovered. The CBC carried the story. So did the *New York Times.* One Australian scientific journal called the Canadian discovery "a masterly account with an abundance of corroborative detail."

It may have been all that, but what it was not, was true. Claude Emile Jean-Baptiste Litre was a boozy April Fool's invention of a couple of folks in the science faculty at Waterloo, a revelation that was not received all that well by the boffins who'd been taken in by the joke. One British science anthology editor who'd swallowed the litre lampoon and written about it sniffed, "It is assumed that communications from established scientists are sincere."

Aw, lighten up, sir. Monsieur Litre should be taken in the same spirit as that poem about your countryman and colleague, Sir Humphry Davy, the famous British scientist. You know the poem?

Sir Humphry Davy
Abominated gravy
He lived in the odium
Of having discovered sodium.

That's a clerihew—from the master himself—Edmund Clerihew Bentley.

And that's that, Tom declared finally.

One Man's Camp Is Another Man's Cottage

We gas a lot about the "true North" here in the Great White You-Know-What, but the truth is, we can't even agree on what North is. Is Parry Sound in the north? Compared to Pangnirtung? What about Barrie?

Well, I can't speak to the national scene but when it comes to telling North from South in Ontario I've got a rule of thumb that's more reliable than an Eagle Scout compass rolled up in a CAA road map.

Flag down the next native you see and ask him where he spends his summer holidays.

If he says, "at camp," you're in the north. If he says, "at the cottage," you're in the nether regions of Ontari-ari-ari-o.

In suburban Toronto, where I grew up, it was always "cottage." You "went to the cottage" for the weekend. You spent your summers "up at the cottage." You caught your big bass "off the dock at Grandpa's cottage."

Camps? Sure, we knew camps. There were Bible camps, Boy Scout camps, Indian camps and Van Camp's pork and beans.

I didn't hear an adult refer to any other kind of camp until I was in my mid-thirties and an ex-Hogtowner-cum-greenhorn newly settled in Thunder Bay.

I remember the moment well. I was getting to know my next-door neighbour, a laconic Finn, over a pot of coffee. He hoisted his mug, took a hearty slurp and then said, "Nagst summer, you comink to our camp for veekent."

Oh dear, I said to myself. What have I moved in next to? A religious fundamentalist? A Nordic Baden-Powell?

Nothing of the sort. Old Yorma was extending the ultimate in northern neighbourliness—an invitation to spend a weekend at his summer place.

Not that a northerner's camp and a southerner's cottage are interchangeable. By and large the northern camp is a good deal rougher and readier than its effete southern cousin. Northerners go to camp for the fishing, the hunting and the solitude—not to play a series of Away Games in the Keeping Up with the Joneses Tournament. You'll see none of your sleek teak and mahogany Ditchburns or Greavette Streamliners lashed to a cleat in front of a northern camp. More likely it'll be a fourteen-foot dinged-in, bunged-up Lund aluminum runabout with a red stripe down its flank. Camp owners tilt toward workhorse boats. Sluggers that can handle everything from uncharted shoals and new-this-year beaver dams to submerged deadheads and premature feeze-ups that put an unexpected half inch of skim ice on the lake.

The camps themselves are far less prettified than the enchanted rustic fantasies you often find in the Muskokas or the Haliburton Highlands. I don't remember seeing too many geranium planters or driveways lined with kitschy painted rocks at camps around the Lakehead. Flagpoles are scarce up there, and so are boat-houses, gazebos and guest cabins.

So which is better, the camp or the cottage? Don't ask this tainted witness. I was brought up on cottages and weaned on camps. I still get tears in my eyes recalling the smell of a Muskoka cottage newly opened in spring . . . two parts kerosene to one part mothball, with a pinch of pine resin and a sprinkle of mouse poop tossed in for seasoning.

On the other hand, I have experienced few finer moments than one I recall sitting on a porch overlooking Lake Superior, watching the bronzed globe of a sinking sun get upstaged by a family of cavorting loons.

Camps and cottages, cottages and camps. They both have their warts and their beauty spots. The season is shorter for camps—and fiercer. The bugs are merciless up north. Only a neophyte or a masochist would venture out to camp unarmed with a bottle of Off, Flit, Musk Oil or (a northern icon) McKirdy's Special Repelfly.

Southern Ontario cottages are much more benign—and don't try to frighten me with sagas of mosquitoes in Muskoka. Compared to Northern Ontario blackflies, they are lap gerbils.

You get fewer surprises at cottages. Such as looking out your kitchen window straight into the beady black button eyes of a foraging momma black bear *avec famille* promenading along your front porch.

On the other hand, northern camps are accessible. Lots of camp owners simply move to their camps for the summer and commute to work. It's only an extra half hour or so. No northerner I know would believe the three-, four- and five-hour chrome-crunching, fender-bending odysseys many Southern Ontarians brave to get to and from their cottages.

Cottage or camp . . . camp or cottage.

I don't care what you call it, I don't have either, and it's been a long hard winter and I can't wait to be invited to one.

Or the other.

A Canuck in the D.R.

A Canadian embarks on a short, sharp midwinter Caribbean vacation with a certain amount of trepidation. Especially if that vacation is to unfold in the Dominican Republic. The D.R., as travel agents like to call it, is not after all, Myrtle Beach or Malibu. It is the eastern two-thirds of the second-largest island in the West Indies, with cloud-shrouded mountain ranges, lizard-green valleys, beaches so white that they hurt the eye, and a Spanish-speaking population still emerging from under the shadow of one of the most brutal dictators ever spawned in an area that grows them like, well, bananas.

Rafael Trujillo ran the Dominican Republic as his personal fiefdom, charnel house and brothel for thirty-one years, until he was thoughtfully blown away by his own military officers in 1961. One hates to say it, but Trujillo makes the case for assassination as a credible political solution. The man was a pig, as well as a thief and a murderer. Washington thought he was swell because he was also anti-Communist.

But that's in the past. Today the Dominican Republic, while not exactly a classical Athenian democracy, is definitely a better place to live for the average Dominican than it was under Trujillo. A big part of the reason for that is tourists. They leave several hundred million dollars on the island every year. The D.R. is keen on tourists.

Canadian tourists particularly. Why Canucks? I'm not sure. Perhaps it's because Dominicans once maintained their own professional baseball team in Canada—the Blue Jays. Maybe it's because from a Dominican perspective Canadians are the ultimate tourists—polite, sun starved and rich. And we are rich. The D.R. makes you very aware of that. Julio, our guide on a tour bus, is asked what the monthly wage is for a Dominican. It depends, he says, on whether you work for the government or for free enterprise. Government employees make a minimum of 400 pesos a month. Under free enterprise they must be paid at least 500 a month.

Several square miles of sugar cane plantation swim by the bus window as the Canadian passengers try to visualize living in Toronto or Trois-Rivières or Tuktoyaktuk on the equivalent of eighty to a hundred Canadian dollars a month.

And what about all that sugar cane out the window? It's virtually an ocean of green that stretches out sometimes from horizon to horizon. "Say, Hoolio, how do ya harvest all this sugar cane?" yells a ruddy-faced farm boy from Georgetown, Ontario. "You got binders? Combines?" "Machete," says Julio. Another large silence.

But the Dominicans are not a mournful lot. If they have been dealt a shabby hand in the economic poker game of twentieth-century global politics, they don't moon over it. They seem remarkably buoyant and unscarred by their lower standard of living. Perhaps it has something to do with living in a sun-splashed tropical paradise where the entire citizenry looks like Tahitian extras from *Mutiny on the Bounty,* manna grows on trees and there is no expression for the term "snow tires."

Not that my entire trip to the Dominican was what you'd call Eden in a hammock. There were long, tedious stretches of what I'd have to call the worst of Banana Republicanism . . . hours spent in crocodile lineups that went nowhere . . . chewing on cold, old, absurdly overpriced pseudofood . . . fretting over disappeared luggage . . . being ignored by surly, lazy natives . . .

Mind you . . . once I got out of Pearson International Airport, everything was fine.

United We Fly

Just occurred to me that lately I've been spending more time in airports than I care to. Not that airports by themselves bother me all that much. My hangup is the traditional method we have of getting from airport to airport. Fear of flying is what I've got.

Well, that's not exactly true, either. I'm pretty well used to flying. My big character flaw is fear of crashing. It starts to show up in the airport waiting lounge. I begin asking myself silly questions like . . . well, take the security scanners. Given that I have to spread-eagle in front of a wand-wielding rent-a-tyrant and try to justify having a metal zipper in my pants, how does a guy with a steel plate in his head ever get through? And other questions like . . . could a pilot, if he was really bored or drunk, or if he had, say, a loose steel plate in his head . . . could he put a 747 through an Immelman turn? Pilots don't have to go through the scanners, of course.

My uneasiness doesn't ease any when I'm finally inside that metal pipe, strapped down like Gulliver into a seat clearly intended for a pre-schooler, being lectured about "loss of cabin pressure," "flotation devices under my seat" and the possibility of "slight turbulence" by immaculately groomed androids with stunningly insincere smiles.

Some people have no such reservations about airplanes. Some

folks are quite the opposite. Some folks are charter members of the Mile High Club, which is to say they have, ah, cemented their bond with a fellow club initiate in the most graphic and intimate way in an airplane at an altitude at or exceeding 5,280 feet above sea level.

Yes, friends, while you and I are white-knuckling our plastic chair tables or trying fruitlessly to wrench the tops off those over-priced perfume bottles of hootch, the passengers in 18B and 18C are both in 18A.

Just such a couple joined the Mile High Club recently on American Airlines Flight 37 from Zurich to San Diego.

Actually this one was a little messier than most initiations. Apparently the flight attendants took umbrage and tried to inter-rupt the ceremony. This understandably vexed the devotees and also some folks across the aisle—"voyeurs" the airline lawyer dubbed them; I prefer to think of them as a rooting section. By the time the plane touched down for a Chicago stopover, there were police cars with winking lights all over the tarmac.

Far as I'm concerned the whole thing is a clear misunderstanding. That couple never should have been on an American Airlines flight.

They were obviously meant to fly United.

Winnie the White River Pooh

If I were a resident of White River, Ontario, I think I'd be wondering about now if my town was afflicted with a case of giant municipal B.O. For some reason, White River can't buy, rent or lease an ounce of respect.

It's a mystery to me. I've been to White River. It's a perfectly respectable hamlet on the Trans-Canada highway, well placed to serve as a pit stop or a wayside rest for anyone who wants a break from jousting with tractor trailers while driving over the north of Superior hump between Thunder Bay and Sault Ste. Marie. Lovely scenery, great fishing, friendly folks—so how come White River gets such shoddy treatment?

First we give it the archival cold shoulder. Can't find White River in the *Canadian Encyclopedia*. Oh, there's room in there for Whitehorse and White Rock and Whiteshell. We included Bob White and Whitefish and White Paper and even White-collar Crime—but White River? Not so much as a preposition.

Then there was the famous White River thermometer—a huge neon billboard by the side of the highway that showed a thermometer festooned with icicles and just a tiny dot of mercury at the bottom. "Welcome to White River," said the legend—"coldest spot in Canada." Stood there for years. People used to take pictures of each other beside that thermometer. You could even buy postcards that showed it.

Then some officious nitpicker in Environment Canada took issue with the White River claim. Said the record wasn't official. The thermometer came down.

You would think that The Bear might have succeeded where the *Canadian Encyclopedia* and the neon thermometer failed. You would think surely The Bear could put White River on the map. The Bear is historical. Goes back to World War I when a Canadian Army lieutenant passing through White River bought a live bear cub from a hunter for $20. He took the bear with him to England. When he found out he was heading for the trenches, the lieutenant gave the bear to the London zoo.

The bear, named Winnipeg by the homesick Canadian soldier, became a star at the London zoo. And nobody loved him more than a little toddler by the name of Chris Milne, even though his preschool tongue had trouble pronouncing the name Winnipeg. Little Christopher just called the bear "Winnie." Fortunately for little Christopher, his father was a writer. Fortunately for all of us, actually. Chris's father was A.A. Milne. He wrote the world-famous Winnie the Pooh books and immortalized the little cub from White River.

Now you would think being the hometown of the most famous bear in English literature would be enough to earn White River a little respect. Town officials thought so, too. They were all set to put up a big statue of Winnie, until the letter from Walt Disney Studios arrived. Disney holds the copyright to Winnie the Pooh. The Disney lawyers said no dice. No statue. Period. So here we have an American owner of a British work saying that Canadians cannot honour an Ontario bear with a Manitoba name.

Free trade. How do you like it so far?

Not Your Usual Well-Groomed Job Applicant

You know what I hate most about working for a living? Getting it. Work, I mean—the job interview. I hate 'em. They make my knees wobble and my throat go dry. They turn me into a lickspittly forelock-tugging (if I had a forelock) toady. Every time I go for a job interview I hear some silly clown telling fatuous lies and outrageous distortions about me, my work background and my ambitions for the future. And, worst insult of all, the swine is using my voice.

Still, even my most horrible job interview went better than Dan Pollock's. I've had some pretty disastrous encounters with personnel managers, but I've never, ever showed up for my interview dripping wet, caked with mud and with seaweed hanging out of my cuffs. Dan Pollock did. In Vancouver not long ago. And he was half an hour late, to boot.

It had already been quite a day for Dan. Just an hour or so earlier he'd been briskly striding along the edge of English Bay when he saw a curious thing. An elderly lady, fully dressed, walking . . . into English Bay. Dan Pollock yelled to her, "Hey, lady, what are you doing?" No answer. She was past her hips and wading deeper. Dan Pollock looked around, yelled some more and then, aw geez, took off his suit coat, dropped it on the sand and waded into the frigid bay waters after her. He got close enough to ask her why she was doing what she was doing. The lady told Pollock that she was old and sick and didn't have a place to live and nobody cared anymore.

"Somebody cares," said Dan Pollock, as he felt cold mud oozing into his shoes and watched the water sog the crease out of his pants. "I care."

But they were both out of their depth now. Pollock was treading water. He wasn't sure he could reach her in time. He swam back to the beach and hailed a passing jogger. The jogger ignored him.

So Pollock slooshed across the beach to a hotel where he convinced a waiter to call the police. By the time Pollock got back to the beach, a couple of police had already arrived and hauled the unconscious woman out of the water. Dripping and shivering, Dan Pollock went back to pick up his suit coat and his umbrella where he'd dropped them—and discovered that while he'd been out in the bay trying to save the suicidal woman, somebody had stolen his wallet. He lost sixty dollars and all his identification.

So that's the Dan Pollock who showed up for the job interview—sopping wet, mud up to his knees, flat broke, unable to produce so much as a driver's licence or a social insurance number—and half an hour late, of course.

To give him credit, Dan Pollock didn't cringe or snivel or make up lies or excuses. He just told the manager what had happened and said he'd like to go home, change and come back later, if that was all right.

It was. He did. And you know what? He was hired. "I got the job," says Dan cheerfully. "Maybe that's the payoff."

Dan's just a kid yet. Doesn't know that for people with an attitude like his, the world is full of payoffs.

Black by Popular Demand

1993

How Much Ya Wanna Bet?

So you think you got what it takes to be a professional gambler, eh, pal? Well, let me give you two pieces of gambling advice. Number one: In pressure games, always bet against the Dallas Cowboys, the Detroit Tigers, and Germany.

That's a tip I got from a gambler. I don't know if it works, but I've been waiting for a chance to say it for years.

My second piece of advice comes from a Damon Runyon story. It's a gambler dad passing along some advice to his would-be gambler son. "Son," he says, "as you go around and about in this world, some day you will come upon a man who will lay down in front of you a new deck of cards with the seal unbroken, and offer to bet he can make the jack of spades jump out of the deck and squirt cider in your ear.

"Son," the old man continued, "do not bet him, because as sure as taxes, if you do, you are going to get an earful of cider."

Okay, you've all heard the disclaimer; everybody's read the warning on the package that says gambling can lead to acute poverty. Now let's have some fun with barroom bets. See this perfectly average paperclip I've got in my hand? Ten bucks says you can't guess, to the nearest half inch, how long it'll be when I straighten it out. Whaddaya figure—inch and a half? Two inches? Two and a half? Nope. Time's up. The answer is four inches, and if you don't believe me wreck a normal paperclip and find out. Oh yeah . . . and you owe me ten bucks.

Little green at barroom bets, are you? Well, don't feel bad, so was Mark Anthony. He really got hustled by Cleopatra. She bet him that she could drink half a million dollars' worth of wine without getting up from the table. The aptly named "Mark" said, "You're on, Cleo." Whereupon Cleopatra pinched two near-priceless pearls from a string around her neck, popped them in her goblet, and chuggalugged to win the bet.

Gotta be careful of barroom bets. They thrive on suckers. And suckers can be on either side of the pot. Like the guy who went into the bar with a parrot on his shoulder and announced loudly, "This parrot can sing 'The Little Drummer Boy' and do all the parts—from the drum riff to the last soprano in the Harry Simeon Chorale. Anybody want to bet I'm wrong?" Bartender looks at him, says, "Okay, pal, I'll take your money." Lays fifty on the bar. Couple other guys along the bar have been listening, they move over and add their money. Pretty soon the bar is carpeted with cash. Parrot owner can barely cover the bets, but he does, then turns to the bird. "Pretty Polly. Polly sing. Little Drummer Boy. Prrrrump pah. Go ahead."

Nothin'. The bird might as well be the Maltese Falcon. The guy is cleaned out. Walking home, he says to the parrot, "What's the matter with you? You humiliated me. You cost me my last dime. Why didn't you sing?"

Parrot says, "Get serious. Think how high the odds are gonna be when we go back in there next week."

Ah, yes. Gambling. Another famous Mark—with the last name Twain—said: "There are two times in a man's life when he should not speculate. When he can't afford it and when he can." Ah, good old Twain. Born in Florida, you know. Was so! Betcha ten bucks.

You lose. Mark Twain (or Samuel Clemens) was born in 1835 in the tiny town of Florida, Missouri.

That's twenty bucks you owe me, pal.

And could you rebend those paperclips before you leave?

Don't Look Now, But This Country's Bugged

And the blackflies, the little blackflies,
Always the blackfly no matter where you go,
I'll die with the blackfly apickin' my bones
In North Ontario-io

—VENERABLE CANADIAN SONG LYRIC

We're on the downslide side of another summer, no question about it—but that's not so bad for humans. The approach of autumn means no more than an extra blanket on the bed for you and me. It's the kiss of death for bugs.

Yep, all those nasty little critters with stingers and buzzers and feelers and altogether too many legs are just one hard frost away from meeting their maker. I am not a bloodthirsty man, but the thought of billions of man-eating bugs clutching their hearts and falling flat on their carapaced backs fills me with joy unalloyed. *DIE, you little #*@*#&'s!* I'm delighted to know that I'll never see you again, and so is the back of my neck.

If there is a heaven, and if I ever get there, I hope there's a Question Period. I can't wait to ask the Chief Product Control Officer why he or she thought a planet (already infested with a surfeit of lawyers, politicians, and the incipient threat of hemorrhoids) needed such a bewildering variety of insects with a taste for human pelt.

Because it isn't just blackflies that want to jump our veins. It's mosquitoes and deer flies and horseflies and mites and gnats and beer bugs and noseeums—all, all of the vampiric persuasion.

And in some parts of this country—everything north of Tecumseh Road in Windsor, Ontario—they hover in clouds, nay, *galaxies* just waiting for some fat, pink, warm-blooded creature in Bermuda shorts to blunder by.

Why so many of them? And what do they do for lunch when they don't have my body to fight over for drilling rights?

I can't prove it, but I suspect if you peeled back the lichens that blanket the floor of Canada's boreal forest, you'd find countless tiny, gothic, Frankensteinian castles each no bigger than a good-sized mosquito welt. And I bet if you could peer into the darkest vault in the miniature dungeons beneath each of those castles, you'd see row after row of eensy-weensy coffins lining the walls.

That's where the bugs live. In those coffins. Just imagine eighty kazillion dwarf Bela Lugosis wearing deely boppers. Until I, like a fool, show up for a camping trip or a barbecue. That's when the bug lookout rings the dinner gong, eighty kazillion tiny coffin lids slide back, and the bugs come after me, buzzing their blood-curdling battle cry: *"Soup's onnnnnnnnn!"*

It's not that grim everywhere in Canada, of course. Insect intensity varies greatly across our Dominion. The mosquitoes that wait in ambush along the shores of Ungava Bay, for instance, are the Exocet missiles of the biting bug world. They make mosquitoes that live and prey along the American border look like limp-mandibled panty-waists. Folks in Vancouver, on the other hand, love to skinny-dip in their hot tubs out on the deck, airily remarking that they "have no mosquitoes to worry about."

Yeah, well, they got Bill Vander Zalm too. Everything evens out.

In any case, it could be worse. We Canucks could be living in Equatorial Africa, watching a Goliath beetle trying to Have His Way with the family Volkswagen in the driveway. Goliath beetles are as big as your hand, tipping the scales at nearly a quarter of a pound.

And I've heard tell of a water-dwelling insect that inhabits certain South American rivers. In between hosts, that is. This critter prefers to live in the urinary tracts of mammals dumb enough to urinate in the river. The bug is extremely heat-sensitive, and small enough to home in on and swim up the urinary tract of larger animals, including humans. The bug lodges in the urinary tract, using spiny fins that open up like an umbrella to keep him there.

The pain, I am told, is in livid Technicolor.

On second thought, Canadian bugs don't seem half bad.

Joyful Sex: The Canadian Position

The Japanese perused pillow books. The Indians studied the Kama Sutra. The Italians learned their lessons from *The Decameron*. The French took their cue from the memoirs of Casanova. And North Americans? North Americans got the *Joy of Sex*. Kind of a *Fanny Hill* as told to Mr. Rogers.

I suppose just about every North American over the age of thirty-five bought, borrowed, or at least thumbed through *The Joy of Sex* back in the early seventies. You know the one, the Gourmet Guide to Lovemaking, Complete and Unabridged, Illustrated Edition, compiled by the serendipitously named Alex Comfort, MB, PhD.

Well, no rest for the wicked, I guess. Dr. Comfort, that randy old rake, has risen to the occasion once more. Now at bookstores everywhere: *JoySex III*—or to give it its proper title: *The New Joy of Sex: A Gourmet Guide to Lovemaking in the Nineties.*

What's new about sex twenty years later? A king Hell sandtrap called AIDS, for one thing. Gotta give Dr. Comfort a few strokes off for daring to bring out a sex manual in an era when a lot of would-be swingers are Just Saying No . . . Thanks.

But *The New Joy of Sex* is nothing if not à la mode. It's even pinched a soupçon of the nationalistic fervour currently sweeping the planet. Poles, Czechs, Albanians, and Latvians demanding their own space? Then, by Eros, the least Doc Comfort can do is make sure they have their own sexual positions to occupy those spaces. Thus in *The New Joy of Sex* we discover acrobatic configurations that even a gymnast like Nadia Comaneci, let alone a cosmopolitan contortionist like Casanova, never dreamed of. The book gives us intimate, full-colour delineation and description of the Indian and Japanese preferred positions. We can also peruse at leisure the Serbian Stance, the Croatian Crouch, and the Hungarian Huddle. Not to mention the lyrical Chinese, who seem to ride a sexual seesaw between Wailing Monkey Clasping Tree and Wild Geese Flying on Their Backs.

There is one glaring omission from *The New Joy of Sex.* I can find nary a line drawing nor rhyming couplet that deals with the Canadian Coital Question. What's the preferred posture here in the Great White North? Bellowing Moose with Trembling Aspen? Shivering Beaver Under Soaring Eagle? Not a jot or a tittle about it in this book.

Never mind the position, what about the romantic setting for Canuck-style cuddling? A loaf of prairie bannock, a jug of Niagara wine, and thou beside me, singing sea shanties in the barren lands? Too predictable.

But dammit all, this is an important question—and one that needs to be answered before Dr. Comfort hits us with *Son of All New More Joy of Sex Four, the Sequel.* The Canadian position—and location—need to be defined!

I know! We'll handle it the Canadian way. First we'll appoint a Royal Commission . . . and then we'll ask Quebec!

Philandering Fauna

*I told my wife the truth: that I was seeing a
psychiatrist. Then she told me the truth: that she was
seeing a psychiatrist, two plumbers, and a bartender.*
—RODNEY DANGERFIELD

Adultery. "A sport created by the marriage system," according to
one cynical wag. A sport that goes back a long way too, apparently. "An ancient and long-established custom ... to set your
neighbour's bed a-shaking." Who wrote that—Harold Robbins?
Erica Jong? Irving Layton?

Nope. Those words were put together by a Roman scribbler by
the name of Juvenal about two thousand years ago.

Oh well, at least the sin of adultery is confined to the human
animal, right? *Homo sapiens* may be an inveterate two-timer, but
the other species on the planet are simple, decent, honest types that
stick with their mates no matter what.

Isn't that what the biology prof, *Reader's Digest,* and all those
Walt Disney movies taught us?

Well, that used to be the way things were, Virginia. Up until
just a few years ago, biologists believed that about 95 percent of all
bird species were nuclear family types, one mother and one father

sharing the burden of raising their brood. Lately, scientists have been looking a little more closely and discovering that those families aren't quite as squeaky-clean as they'd first thought.

In fact, they now estimate that up to a third of the birds in any given nest were probably sired by a, as the saying goes, "non-resident male."

And it's not just our feathered friends who are afflicted with the roving eye. Scientists have been shadowing rabbits, elk, and ground squirrels more closely than ever before.

Same story, basically. They've found that the aforementioned species fool around a lot more than we ever thought they did—and what's more, it's the females who usually initiate the debauchery.

As often as not, the male is reduced to a helpless, blustering cuckold, storming around kicking pine cones and cursing his in-laws while his inamorata is out painting the forest red with some other stud.

The male Idaho ground squirrel is particularly pathetic. When his mate is in heat, the male dogs her tirelessly right around the clock. He'll even chase her down a hole and sit on top of it to keep her away from any passing curly-tailed Casanovas.

As for birds, the experts are having trouble finding *any* feathered species that lives up to the old Puritan ethic. Even tiny chickadees, those chirpy, Audrey Hepburnish innocents who spend the winters with us, are not, it seems, immune to an illicit roll in the snow.

Philandering is rampant in the so-called animal world. Patricia Gowaty, a biologist at Clemson University, South Carolina, says, "It seems that all our old assumptions are incorrect."

Mind you, there may be a perfectly sound biological reason for all the extramarital matings these critters get up to. Experts theorize that the females may be ensuring that their eggs get fertilized by a variety of male donors, thus guaranteeing genetic diversity in her offspring.

Unlike humans, they don't do it just for fun.

Reminds me of the story of the old general who, off to the wars, locked his young wife in a chastity belt and gave the key to his best friend. "If I'm not back in a year, release my wife," said the general, and then he set off. That night in camp the general looked up to see his best friend galloping up to his tent. "General," he gasped, "you gave me the wrong key."

Don't Judge a Livre by Its Cover

Ever been really, totally, utterly humiliated? Yeah, me too. I'm far too polite to ask about your experience, and still way too embarrassed to talk publicly about mine . . . so a compromise. I'll tell you all about Peter Van Harten's totally humiliating experience. Peter was a guy I went to school with. We also spent some time hoofing through Europe together. Now, Peter had a lot of swell personal attributes, but linguistic fluidity was not one of them. When it came to communicating in a foreign language, Peter might as well have been a goldfish.

I can see now that it was a terrible mistake to send him alone into that little grocery store in Calais. Get some eggs for breakfast, Pete, we told him. Les oeufs, s'il vous plait—that's all you have to say. And hold out your money.

Alas, Peter tried to finesse it. One should never try to finesse the French. Finesse is their business. Heck, finesse is their word.

"Ge vooks," announced Van Harten to the French grocer, "dez oofs de la pool . . ."

And that's as far as he got. A warp speed torrent of machine-gun French riding on a high, keening shriek erupted from the throat of Mme Defarge behind the counter. I didn't catch all of her rant as she drove Van Harten out into the street with her broom, but I know I heard "Quelle atroce!"—what an atrocity. There were some bits about never darkening doorways and barbarians from abroad too.

Well, the French are like that, eh? They love the language and they fuss and fret over the words of their language, treating them like preemies. Is there any other country that has a full-blown Academy meeting annually to decide whether new words are worthy enough to be admitted into the language? France does. A woman I know says she got a lot of glares whenever she spoke French in Paris. Which was disconcerting for her because she was from Trois-Rivières and had been speaking French all her life.

The French feel culturally superior to all mere mortals and make no bones about it. For years they've snickered at boorish Americans, patronized Québécois bumpkins, and twitted the Brits for their sang-froid. You just knew that they considered the rest of us unlettered brutes, and why not? Didn't our own literary standard-bearers—Callaghan and Hemingway and Joyce and Pound—answer the siren call of the Paris cafés? Ah, yes. France must truly be the most literary nation in the history of mankind.

Or so we all assumed until a study commissioned by the French ministry of culture came out. It shows that three-quarters of the French adults surveyed had never attended a classical music concert; over half had never seen a play, and two-thirds of them hadn't read *any* books recently.

Surprised? Me too. Serves us right, I guess, for making cultural assumptions about folks we don't know all that well. Reminds me of the story of an embassy dinner in Washington where a young American society woman sitting next to a Chinese dignitary tried to start a conversation by pointing to the entree and saying, "Likee soupee?" The man nodded. After the meal the Chinese dignitary was asked to address the guests. Which he did. For ten minutes. In flawless English. Returning to his seat amid applause, he murmured to the young woman, "Likee speechee?"

Fractured English

Here is a letter from a grumpy reader that begins, "I have been several times surprised at your careless use of English, but you have outdone yourself in this . . ." And the letter goes on to flay me for an alleged linguistic misdemeanour.

All I can say to Grumpy Reader is, for God's sake, sir, obtain a life. If you have nothing better to do than pore over my poor prose winnowing out grammatical offences, then you are a man in serious need of a hobby.

Have you considered tatting?

Mind you, he has a point. English grammar and I have had little more than a nodding acquaintance since those dreary, dreadful days of Grade 7 English composition, when a merciless Miss Swinson lashed the class with volley upon volley of English Grammar Rules and Regs.

It made me the pathetic, unlettered wretch I am today. Even now, I shamble around with my participles dangling obscenely, tripping over misplaced modifiers, slapping ineffectively at insubordinate nouns, averting my eyes shyly from those brazen copulative conjunctions that don't even have the common decency to wear a set of brackets . . .

It's a situation up with which no one should have to put.

And sometimes I can't—put up with it, I mean. When that happens I have a failsafe cure. I reach for my Fractured English file.

This is where I keep my collection of pieces by people who mangle the English language even more grievously than I (do). More often than not, these folks are labouring under a disadvantage—namely, that English is clearly not their first language.

Such as whoever wrote this brochure for a Japanese car rental firm. Some advice it offers: "When a passenger of foot heave in sight, tootle the horn. Trumpet at him melodiously at first, but if he still obstacles your passage, then tootle him with vigour."

Or these assembly instructions that came with an Italian-made baby carriage: "Insert the blushing for blocking in the proper split, push it deeply and wheel in anti time sense till it stops."

Oh yes, and *buona fortuna.*

A polite reminder on the back of a Japanese hotel room door is, I think, appropriately Zen-like: "Is forbitten to steal the hotel towels please. If you are not person to do such thing, is please not to read notis."

In the Scandinavian countries, English is often spoken, but not always flawlessly. Witness the Oslo cocktail lounge that sports a sign reading: "Ladies are requested not to have children in the bar."

Riding in elevators can be unnerving in the most cosmopolitan of cities, but there's one lift in Belgrade that I intend to avoid for the rest of my life. It carries a sign that reads in (sort of) English: "To move the cabin, push button for wishing floor. If the cabin should enter more persons, each one should press number of wishing floor. Driving is then going alphabetically by national order."

Under which some wag has crayoned: "Or you could take the stairs."

Sometimes overseas English isn't merely mangled—it's fraught with menace. Look at this advertisement in a Hong Kong dentist's window. It reads: "Teeth extracted by the latest Methodists."

Or the sign in a Jordanian tailor shop that advises: "Order your summer suit. Because is big rush we will execute customers in strict rotation."

Or the notice on the wall of an Acapulco hotel dining room: "The management has personally passed all the water served here."

No wonder they warn *turistas* not to drink the water.

Judicious English

Somebody once defined a judge as a person of few words but many sentences. Well, you can read that verdict any way you like. The fact is that judges—and justice in general—remain firmly in the realm of mystery for most of us.

I think language is largely to blame. The system of jurisprudence that governs our lives springs from a bedrock of Latin. Now that was hunky-dory when young scholars lapped up Latin and Greek at the feet of their school instructors. Nowadays, kids are more likely to be taking advanced computer graphics and conversational Mandarin. People are moving along with the times. But the law clings tenaciously to its Latin roots. Now, Latin may or may not be a dead language, but it's certainly buried. Which becomes a problem when life throws one of its wicked split-fingered fastballs at us and we find ourselves in a court of law. Suddenly the air is full of *ipso factos* and *flagrante delictos*. We hear strangers droning on about *mandamus* and *mittimus*. They tell us it's a case of Regina *versus* Black and it will be held *in camera*.

And most of us don't have a clue what they're talking about.

Jim Carnwath is somebody who would like to change all that by bringing our judicial system into the twentieth century, linguistically speaking. And that's good news for the rest of us, because Jim Carnwath is a Provincial Court judge.

Each year Judge Carnwath drives down to London, Ontario, for a couple of weeks in the summer and stands up in front of a classroom, not a courtroom, of fellow judges. And that's when Judge Carnwath really begins his mission: to teach his colleagues to speak English.

Common, ordinary, over-the-back-fence, down-at-the-Legion-Hall English. Mostly he's trying to get the judges to shed their fondness for abstruse windiness and stuffy legalisms. He encourages them to forgo intoning "cease and desist" when what they mean is "stop." As he puts it: "Who would ever come home for dinner and say, 'I'd like another piece of that raspberry pie. Said pie was the best you ever made.'?"

He tells them to get rid of the *ab initio*—the phrase "in the beginning" is much clearer. Similarly, he tells the judges to stop referring to the *actus reus* when what they mean is "the criminal act."

More power to Judge Carnwath, I say. Still, I hope he doesn't take all the wind out of those judges' linguistic sails. There are occasions when judicial obfuscation is called for. Such as the time one Alberta circuit court judge had to write to a British couple informing them that their young son had been found guilty and hanged for cattle rustling. The judge didn't *have* to be compassionate, but he saw no reason to compound the parents' grief by telling them their son had ended a dissolute life at the end of a rope. So he took plumed pen in hand and wrote: "Please accept my condolences on the loss of your son. His youth was cruelly snatched from him when a platform on which he was standing suddenly gave way."

Not strictly honest, perhaps . . . but judicious in the finest sense of the word.

Stompin' Tom for Poet Laureate

How beautifully useless,
how deliciously defiant
a poem is!

—RAYMOND SOUSTER

Tell the truth, now—when's the last time you picked up a book of poetry?

Yeah. Me too. I manage to wade through *Maclean's, Saturday Night,* the *Globe and Mail,* my local paper—even a novel or two each week. But poetry? Sorry, no time.

Part of the reason is of course that much modern poetry is so infuriatingly inaccessible. Here, for instance, is the last gasp of the final stanza of a Joe Rosenblatt poem about a housefly:

BUZZZZZZZ
BUZZZZZZ
BUZZZZZ
BUZZZZ
BUZZ
BUZ
ZZ
Z

That may be tremendously meaningful to Joe Rosenblatt. It may even be kinda fun to watch him "perform" it at, say, the Hamilton Steelworkers Annual Christmas Party.

But Shakespeare it ain't.

A lot of modern poetry seems to be little more than cerebral foreplay between the author and his or her consciousness. Too bad. As Robertson Davies says, "Poetry is undoubtedly a serious business . . . but the world also needs its entertainers, its bards, who remind us that poetry was not always a question of printed pages, hidden meanings, and dismal intellectual gropings; there was a time when poetry was for everybody, and had some fun in it."

I think Joseph Brodsky would second that. Mr. Brodsky is a Soviet émigré, kicked out of the USSR twenty years ago because his poems infuriated the Politburo. Brodsky picked himself up, dusted himself off, and moved to the US. Eventually the Americans honoured him with the title of US poet laureate.

Brodsky is an old-style poet. The kind who thinks poems ought to be read by everyone, not just weedy academics and neo-Beatnik wannabes.

And he just might do something about it. Brodsky told a Washington audience recently that poetry ought to be sold in supermarkets and left in every motel room, right next to the Gideon Bible. "The Bible won't mind this," he explained. "It doesn't mind being next to the telephone book."

He'd also like to see racks of poetry books available at the corner drugstore. "Poems are cheaper than tranquillizers, and reading them may reduce the bill from your shrink." Rising to the moment, Brodsky declared, "Poetry is perhaps the only insurance we've got against the vulgarity of the human heart, and it should be available to everyone at low cost."

Well, it's not an entirely original thought. One of our own poets, Irving Layton, once wrote, "If the walls that separate people from people are ever pulled down, it will not be done by politicians or dictators. It will be done by poets."

I don't think it would hurt if we broadened our definition of "poet" either. Bruce Cockburn is a Canadian poet. So are k.d. lang, Gordon Lightfoot, Rita MacNeil . . . and Wayne Gretzky.

That's not an original thought either. One of Brodsky's ex-compatriots, Yevgeny Yevtushenko, once visited these shores and announced, "I say the best Canadian poet is Phil Esposito." Then he added thoughtfully, "And that is not a joke."

I say: Stompin' Tom Connors for Canadian poet laureate.

And I'm only joking a little bit.

Tabloids and Ethics: A Natural Oxymoron

You cannot hope to bribe or twist,
Thank God! the British journalist.
But seeing what the man will do
Unbribed, there's no occasion to.

—HUMBERT WOLFE

Sometimes I think I'd like to visit England just for the thrill of strolling down to a London newspaper kiosk and browsing through the morning headlines. One of the few fine remaining pleasures of life in that sad and shabby kingdom is the range of newspapers you can peruse. For a modest mittful of newpence you can take your choice of anything from the august London *Times* at the upscale end all the way down to scuzzy, unspeakable typographical excrescences like the *Mirror* and the *Sun*. For a journophile like yours truly, reading the British press is like living in a lovely English garden overlooking a garbage dump.

The best of British journalism is unquestionably very good indeed. But the worst, my dears, is among the very worst in the world. If you haven't stained your fingers on a typical British tabloid, then you don't know how low the fourth estate can stoop. Canadian tabloids are flashy, irreverent, and occasionally outrageous, but

Canadian tabs are to British tabs as a Brownie pack is to the Mongol hordes.

Few institutions can be as mindlessly chauvinistic or stupefyingly sexist as a British tabloid newspaper in full screech. They flay the royal family unmercifully, insinuating that Prince Charles is an airhead and Princess Margaret a souse. They publish full-page photos of naked nymphets, complete with slavering, sleazy captions about "Luscious Lily's garden of natural delights." There are five basic staples for a classic British tabloid item: sex, soccer, sex, scandal, and sex. And if you can throw in a pinch of aristocratic philandery, you've got yourself a front-page byline, mate.

All of which made me do a serious double take when I saw this headline in my non-British, non-tabloid copy of the *Globe and Mail*. U.K. TABS SIGN ETHICS CODE, it read.

British tabloids? An ethics code? That's like Mike Tyson becoming a Buddhist.

Under the new code, British newspapers will have to justify their intrusions into private lives, mistakes will be acknowledged in print with the same prominence the original items enjoyed, and henceforth editors will no longer pay criminals, their families, or their associates for rights to their "stories."

All of which sounds very laudable, but adherence to the code is strictly voluntary. There's no law that will force any newspaper to actually follow through and obey the code.

You will forgive an old cynic for suspecting that it will be a frosty Friday on Fleet Street before the editors of the *Sun* or the *Mirror* send their reporters out with the gentle admonition to be fair, gentle, and upright at all times.

I prefer to believe that the British press will continue to offer the bewildering and occasionally revolting kaleidoscope of journalism that it has always served up. A full spectrum—good, bad, and ugly—that has been deftly summarized in this excerpt from the book *Yes, Prime Minister,* by Jonathan Lynn and Anthony Jay:

> The *Times* is read by the people who run the country. The *Daily Mirror* is read by the people who think they run the country. The *Guardian* is read by the people who think

they ought to run the country. The *Morning Star* is read by people who think the country ought to be run by another country. The *Independent* is read by people who don't know who runs the country but are sure they're doing it wrong. The *Daily Mail* is read by the wives of the people who run the country. The *Financial Times* is read by the people who own the country. The *Daily Express* is read by the people who think the country ought to be run as it used to be run. The *Sun*'s readers don't care who runs the country provided she has big boobs.

Dirty Hairy

I'll bet you were asking yourself, "Gee, I wonder what's new in hair these days."

Well, sit'cherself down in my visitor's barber chair here, friend . . . you've come to the right place. I am a hair veteran. Been there and gone. I've lived through, if not actually cultivated: crew cuts, brush cuts, Iroquois cuts, college cuts, Beatle cuts, shag cuts, and Curly, Larry, and Moe cuts. I've seen my fellow man wear his hair in ponytails and Indian braids; in pompadours and the infamous D.A.—in which young males in heat did their level best to make the back of their heads look like a mallard's behind. The roof I live under may be thatchless now, but it's seen me through the Dry Look, the Wet Look, and the Eight Pounds of Wildroot Cream Oil Charlie Look, in which otherwise sane young men gobbed enough gunk on their locks to grease the retractable roof of the SkyDome.

Oh, I know hair. I've lived through spells of long hair, short hair, no hair, and purple hair. But even I, after a lifetime of tonsorial trend-spotting, would never have predicted the Age of . . . Dirty Hair.

It's true. The latest hairstyle rage is unwashed hair. Not unwashed forever. A couple of weeks, say. Just long enough to give it that lank, shingly look of a fur-bearing rodent drowning in a vat of Mazola. Dirty hair.

Why would anybody do that to the top of his head? To be trendy, of course. California hairdresser Victor Vidal explains, "The whole look is eroticism. It's very animalistic. It's aggressive." One of Mr. Vidal's hairstyling colleagues puts it more simply: "It's a look," he says, "that says, 'Hey, I ride a Harley.'"

Or at least sleep under one with a leaky crankcase.

But what about people who've been, pardon the pun, conditioned to shampooing regularly, yet still want to be "with it," hirsutely speaking? Not to worry, California capitalism is way ahead of you. Enter Molding Mud, a new hair gel that's guaranteed to make clean hair look dirty. A woman by the name of Jerl Cusenza is the inventor of Molding Mud. She says she got her inspiration from a homeless woman pushing a shopping cart through the streets of Los Angeles. "I looked at this girl," says Ms. Cusenza, "and I thought, that's just the kind of separation I want. You know how street people don't wash their hair, and it has this wonderful greasy texture?"

Couldn't agree more. I've always suspected homeless people just do their hair like that for effect.

Molding Mud is selling like, well, like Wildroot Cream Oil used to sell. Selling like hotcakes, but not to me, I'm afraid. I'm coasting as always, a little ahead of the Hair Wave. I'm in another dimension, beyond dirty hair, long hair, short hair, purple hair. I dwell in the Zen-like realm of . . . no hair. No gels for me. Or sprays or conditioners or shampoos.

Mind you, for really special occasions I may use just a dab of Mop & Glo.

Black in the Saddle Again

1996

Felonious Follies

The most common question people ask when they find out that I scribble for a living is "where do you get your ideas?"

I always tell them that I steal them. Which is true. I steal my column ideas from books, magazines, TV programs, things I see on the street, conversations I deliberately overhear in the supermarket.

Unfortunately, sometimes even theft isn't enough. Every once in a while, a guy will find himself hunched over his word processor, a deadline dangling like a Damoclean switchblade over his neck, his fingers poised like twitchy talons over the keyboard and . . .

Nothing.

No inspiration, no ideas—not even the ghost of a notion to fill the blank gaze of the monitor before him.

Scary . . . but all is not lost.

There's always the Dumb Crooks file to fall back on.

It's a manila folder that I keep beside my desk, bulging with news clippings about ruined robberies, fouled-up felonies, heists gone haywire, and gormless gangsters gang agley.

The daily papers are full of them—tiny little "filler" stories about would-be crooks whose walk on the wild side turned into a pratfall.

Such as? Well, such as the story out of Fort Erie, Ontario. A woman working late in an accounting office looked up to see a man armed with a club. He demanded money, then ordered the woman to get into her car.

She did.

He waited for her to unlock the passenger door.

She didn't.

Instead, the woman drove straight to the police station. The cops immediately issued a bulletin in which the details were a bit sketchy.

Officers were alerted to be on the lookout for a man who was "not too swift."

Speaking of Not Too Swift—how about Donald M. Thomas? Mister Thomas escaped from jail in California after serving eighty-nine days.

Of a ninety-day sentence.

He was captured. He now faces up to twenty years in prison.

Ah, yes, but he'll go down as a Legend of Crime. The Birdbrain of Alcatraz.

And let us never forget the famous Edmonton Two—a couple of Albertan Butch and Sundance wannabes who made Canadian criminal history of a sort the night they knocked over the Petro-Canada gas station just outside Vancouver. They surprised the attendant, tied him up, and left him in the washroom, and then escaped with the contents of the till.

But they were, as I say, from Edmonton, and a little bewildered by the bright lights of Vancouver. Which is why, twenty minutes later, they pulled into a gas station to ask directions.

A . . . Petro-Canada . . . gas station.

The same Petro-Canada station they'd knocked over earlier.

The station attendant, just removing the last of the ropes from his ankles, looked up to see his worst nightmare happening all over again. "I guess they didn't recognize me or the station."

He stammered out directions, then quickly called the cops. Just as he was hanging up, the attendant looked up and saw . . .

the same two guys coming toward him.

Their car wouldn't start. Could the mechanic . . . ? Alas, the mechanic wouldn't be on duty until 8:00 a.m.

The Edmonton Two were waiting for a tow truck when a police cruiser pulled in and graciously offered them a free ride downtown.

Let's give the last word to Thomas Russell in the San Joaquin County Jail. Mister Russell, who was doing time for burglary, was startled to receive a government cheque for $26,447. Startled, but not paralyzed. He immediately used $6,500 to post his own bail and promptly left town with the remaining twenty grand.

Which no doubt really ticked off the San Joaquin County tax collector. He'd sent the cheque to the wrong Thomas Russell.

Not exactly a story of dumb crooks, you say? True.

But the bad guys have to win one once in a while.

On the Job

"Work" . . . what a funny word when you think about it. Not that much different from the ancient "verk"—which some acquisitive Anglo-Saxon copped from the Old Norse language several hundred years ago.

Strange word for a strange concept. Some pretty good minds have tried to define the phenomenon. The philosopher Bertrand Russell declared that there are only two kinds of work. Number one: altering the position of matter at or near the earth's surface, relative to other matter. And number two: telling other people to do it. Ogden Nash nailed down another important work characteristic. "People who work sitting down," observed Nash, "get paid more than people who work standing up."

Unless you happen to work at hitting baseballs for a living.

You wouldn't think a four-letter epithet like work could cradle so many contradictions. We've got works of art, bridgework, men at work, work to rule, off work. That's the really weird thing about work. We mumble and moan endlessly about having to go to work . . . while secretly praying that we'll never be out of it.

What is this human foible? Antelope don't work. Turkey vultures make their own hours. Your weeniest microbe may be voteless and unsexy and not very bright—but at least it doesn't have to go to work for a living.

Not like we do. Nine to five, day shift, night shift, time and a half for overtime, forty hours a week, forty-eight weeks a year, not counting Christmas, New Year's, and statutory holidays.

Very odd. Most of us spend better than half our waking hours "at work," and getting to and from it, for five of the seven days we get each week. Which is to say we work more than we sleep or eat or read or make love or hang out with friends.

And why is it we are doing this again? I keep forgetting. Oh right, to become wealthy so we don't have to work. Well, I don't know about you but I've been at it pretty steadily for four decades, and wealth has never been further off. I had more money in my pocket when I was a pin boy at the bowling alley.

Work. We gripe and we groan about it; we shirk and slough it off and try to get out of as much of it as we can, but my, don't we wax self-righteous when we see somebody who's managed to hack-saw their way free of the work ethic ball and chain?

Welfare bums. Pogey cheats. Shiftless good for nothings. HEY YA BUM . . . GET A JOB!

The writer Richard Needham had a theory about that. "If you enjoy your work," he wrote, "you don't mind other people not working; in fact, you're happy to support them. But if, like most Canadians, you hate your work, you resent seeing anybody idle. You want everyone to be as miserable as you are."

Aha. That's the cushy job we're all looking for, of course. Once you like what you're doing, it stops being work. Archibald Lampman put it quite elegantly: "Work is only toil when it is the performance of duties for which nature did not fit us, and a congenial occupation is merely serious play."

But what about the dignity of labour? Summed up nicely, I think, in an anecdote they tell about JFK when he was campaigning for the presidential nomination in West Virginia, back in 1960. At one stop, Kennedy was confronted by a hollow-eyed man, all bone and gristle and coal smudges—obviously a miner. "It true yore the son o' one of ar richest men?" the miner demanded. Kennedy nodded, warily. "True you never wanted for anythin' and had everythin' you wanted?" continued the miner, his eyes boring in.

"I guess so," admitted Kennedy.

"It true you never done a day's work with yore hands all the days of yore life?" accused the miner.

Kennedy nodded guiltily again.

"Well let me tell you somethin', son," growled the miner. "You . . . haven't missed a thing."

Batman Exposed!

Ever wakened from a dead sleep to a saucer-eyed awareness that you were not alone in your bedroom? We did. Last Thursday. Yours truly and my Helpmeet Against Life's Trials, Lynne. Spooky. We didn't hear drawers sliding open or jewellery chinking, or stealthy footsteps padding across the floor. It was more like something just over the threshold of sound . . . like balled-up Kleenexes being lobbed around the room. Then we heard a whispering *thppp thppp*. At the bottom of the bed? Over by the dresser?

But the sound was gone, almost before it registered. We stared into the black but saw nothing—or wait! No, must have been blinking. But there it is again! Just a whiplash across the retina, faster than a politician's smile.

Then I knew. It wasn't a burglar we had in our bedroom. It was a bat.

There's a critter that sure got short-changed in English. Bat. What a pathetically inadequate name. The Aztecs called them butterfly mice. In French they're *chauve souris*—bald mice. The Germans have the best name of all: *Fledermaus*. That's the one we Anglos could have stolen! We could have called them Flittermice. But no . . . we stuck them with the mundane, monosyllabic "bat."

My bedroom intruder was just a little brown bat, but cute as he was and Harrowsmithy as I like to think I am, it's tough to doze off knowing that something that looks like a miniature crime crusader is barrel-rolling through airspace not all that far from your pillow.

Which is why I got up, nude, at 2:30 Thursday morning and put on my duck boots. So I could go out in the backyard shed and rummage through my fishing stuff, and find my old landing net. And okay, I admit it, while I was out there I picked up my bicycle helmet, too, because, well, bats are skittish and they have teeth and claws and I wouldn't want him to mistake my head for a runway or anything.

It's not easy to catch a bat in even a good-sized landing net, but I did it. Well, truth to tell he flew into the net while I was adjusting my chin strap. Point is, I got the bat in the landing net and took him out in the backyard at 2:37 a.m., in the nude, in my duck boots. And I was just kind of holding the netted bat out in front of me and trying to remove the mesh from his wings with a hockey stick, because I didn't want to get too close to a ticked-off bat—even with my bicycle helmet on. And I just about had him free when . . . I hear the car door slam.

My next-door neighbours coming home from a party. So close I could hear their house keys rattling. No sweat, I said to myself. I'll just stand perfectly still. It's dark. They won't see me.

Nor would they have, if my boon companion and pillar of strength against Life's buffeting, Lynne, hadn't chosen that moment to throw on the backyard floodlights. "Need some light dear?" I heard her call cheerily.

No, not really. A black hole would be nice. Or perhaps a cyanide lozenge . . .

The bat flew off. I wished that I could. And my neighbours? You know, I don't know what my neighbours made of it. Haven't seen or heard a peep out of them since Thursday morning.

Not surprised really. Last time I saw them they were looking at me like I had . . .

flittermice in my belfry.

Long John Silver Was a Wimp

Don't talk to me. Don't even look at me. I'm in a bad mood.

I've just had one of my all-time favourite myths pulverized like a sea biscuit under Long John Silver's peg leg.

That's the very myth I mean—pirates. It probably indicates a mutant chromosome in my genetic balance sheet, but I've always had a perverse fascination with pirates. I liked pirates because in a world of shifting values, weasel words, and fake imagery—pirates were, at least, real.

Real . . . *bad.*

The baddest, in fact. Nastier than Nazis and more ruthless than lawyers, even. Pirates had no redeeming features. We're talking about thugs who stalked fat, unarmed merchant ships. Who gloated as they slaughtered unarmed crews and passengers. Who boozed and raped and pillaged and plundered and sent anyone who stood in their way for a long stroll off a short plank, right?

Nah. Not even close.

Fact is, we can thank Robert Louis Stevenson and J.M. Barrie for most of the "truths" we know about pirates. Robert Louis Stevenson wrote *Treasure Island.* J.M. Barrie gave us *Peter Pan.*

But based on historical records, it looks like Messrs. Stevenson and Barrie probably couldn't tell a pirate cutlass from a pork cutlet.

First, the famous skull and crossbones flag. Everybody knows that pirates invariably hoisted the old S&C when they were bearing down on some hapless treasure-laden galleon, right? Wrong. Pirates flew red flags, black flags, flags with full skeletons—in short, any damn flags they pleased. For the most part, they ran up the flag of Utmost Convenience. In other words, if a British frigate was their prey, they flew the Union Jack. If it was a French sloop they had in their sights, they made sure the fleur-de-lis was fluttering in the breeze.

The better to bamboozle the quarry, my pretties.

What about the plank, then? Surely the stories about pirates prinking captives off a plank into the briny are true? Not according to Hugh Rankin, author of *The Golden Age of Piracy*. Ye olde plankwalk, writes Rankin, "appears to have been a fabrication of later generations." Rankin says that when pirates wished to rid themselves of enemies, they simply tossed them over the rail—without benefit of diving board.

Turns out that even among themselves, pirates weren't the lawless band of savages we've come to know and loathe. Buccaneer politics weren't anything like the anarchic seadog-eat-seadog frenzy one might have assumed. It was more like . . . well, the United Nations.

David Cordingly is the organizer of an exhibition on pirate history at the National Maritime Museum in London, England. According to him, inter-pirate behaviour was surprisingly charitable. "Pirates were extraordinarily democratic," he says. "Plunder had to be shared out equally. The captain could take a bit more, but not a lot more, unlike the Navy. A pirate crew could even vote their captain out of office."

Cordingly claims that pirates even operated a kind of High Seas Health Plan—losing a leg in battle, for example, guaranteed a bigger share of the booty.

And here's the kicker for me. Care to meet two of the bloodthirstiest pirates of all time? One was a fearless cutthroat named Read; the other, a sadistic swashbuckler named Bonny. Read and Bonny roamed the seas in the early 1700s, separately at first, then together on an English pirate ship under Calico Jack Rackham. Finally, in 1721 a Jamaican warship tracked them down and after a vicious battle in which Read and Bonny were the last to yield, they captured the pirate sloop and threw the whole crew in chains.

The entire crew was tried, found guilty, and hanged. With the exception of Read and Bonny. They were excused.

They were pregnant. Bonny's first name was Anne; Read's was Mary.

Sure throws cold water on the pirate legend. On the other hand, it opens a whole new career option for Sheila Copps.

Justice by the Handful

I hear rumours that Clint Eastwood plans to do another *Dirty Harry* movie.

I can't pretend that I'm surprised. It must be easy work. When he portrays that ne'er-do-well, rogue San Francisco detective, Harry Callaghan, all Clint has to do is squint a lot, adjust his sunglasses from time to time, and blow away bad guys with his .44 Magnum.

I can't say that I'm surprised, either, that *Dirty Harry* movies continue to be box-office dynamite. They flog the same commodity offered by the *Death Wish* movies Charles Bronson sleepwalks through every couple of years—simple, Old Testament solutions to modern problems. In the worlds of *Death Wish* and *Dirty Harry,* the lesson is always cut and dried and the bad guys are always badder than bad. They're scum: ergo, gun them down.

Would that real life were so simple. Would that modern justice were even in the ballpark.

The other day, on my TV, Oprah was interviewing a prison inmate who had just been sentenced for dealing heroin.

"What did the judge give you?" Oprah asked.

"Eighteen years," said the prisoner.

"And when do you get out?" pursued Oprah.

"I'm eligible for parole next summer," the prisoner replied.

And the TV audience *laughed!* That's how cynical we've become about the courts and justice.

That's why a little cheer leaps unbidden to the back of our throats when we see Dirty Harry short-circuit a legal system that's constipated to the point of immobility. Hooray—here comes simple, monosyllabic Harry dispensing instant "justice" in lethal lead capsules. It's stupid. It's fantasy. But it works.

And the news we get from the courts doesn't seem calculated to make Six Gun Justice any less attractive. Some time ago, I wrote about the despondent New Yorker who tried to kill himself by jumping in front of a subway train. He lived—albeit as a quadriplegic. When he recovered sufficiently, the would-be suicide sued the New York Transit Authority for a million dollars, claiming the Authority had failed to protect him.

He won, too.

Not long ago, a woman sued the Chicago rapid transit system over the death of her husband. And how had he died, exactly? Well, while waiting for his train, he urinated over the tracks.

Right on the electrified rail.

The wife sued for neglect, claiming $1.5 million would go a long way toward allaying her grief.

She also won.

Ah, but every so often the universe unfolds the way it ought to. I give you the tale of a would-be Mississippi rapist. One night a man broke into a house in Jackson and found himself in the bedroom of a fifty-year-old unprotected woman.

Perfect!

He jumped on the woman, slapped her around, cursed her, and when he had her thoroughly frightened, took off his clothes. Which is when the woman grabbed him in what would have been an intimate embrace if it hadn't been quite so . . . energetic.

There are no names in jiu-jitsu for the hold the woman put on the man. You won't see it employed by members of the World Wrestling Federation. Suffice to say it was two-handed, vice-like, and extremely painful.

"Please, please," the man whimpered, "you're killing me!"

"Die, then," the woman said.

"Woman, you got me suffering," he moaned.

"Have you thought about how you were going to leave me suffering?" she replied. With a twist.

The would-be rapist eventually managed to break free and get away, but he wasn't hard to find. Police just followed the crawl marks in the dirt, which led right to his house. They found him in bed, in great pain.

I don't know how Dirty Harry would feel about it, but a story like that sure makes my day.

Holidays for the Politically Correct

Don't look now, folks, but trick-or-treating could be just a little trickier this year. Political correctness has come to Halloween. Yessir . . . the Language Police have cordoned off the centuries-old festivity and declared it ripe for sanitizing. According to a group called the Equity-Affirmative Advisory Committee, there are some costumes your children should not dress up in because said costumes could cause "unpleasant and/or hurtful situations."

So what should your kids *not* dress up as this year? Here's the list: Gypsy. Native Indian. East Indian. Elderly Person. Disabled Person. Slave. Witch. Hobo. Devil.

I see. Yes, fine. Well, that leaves, ahh . . . pretty well nothing, actually. I guess the kids could still dress up as the Maytag Repair Man or a fire hydrant or a largish root vegetable, but I can't see a lot of enthusiasm for those options. Maybe we should just keep the kids indoors on Halloween singing rounds of "Solidarity Forever."

Call me old-fashioned, but I find it hard to imagine a Halloween without clutches of pint-sized devils and witches and hoboes and goblins skittering across my front porch, Unicef boxes in hand. What is it exactly that we're protecting them from?

Well, everything it seems. Even criticism by their peers. There's a principal of a public school down in Weymouth, Massachusetts, who's made the ultimate affirmative action proposal to his school board. Mandatory clapping. John Dowling, principal of East Intermediate Secondary School, wants to make it compulsory for audiences to clap at the end of all auditorium performances—good, fair, or dismal.

"If you get a ten-year-old girl who's singing her heart out, we'd like to see the children clapping, whether she's good or not." And he adds, "We have written standards for other types of behaviour, so why not the same for auditorium behaviour?"

Oh, brave, new, automatically affirming world! Why even put the dear wee ones through the trauma of performance? Why not just a continuous tape loop of thunderous applause broadcast over the public address system from roll call to lights out?

Sure. And once we've exorcised the evils of Halloween, let's go after the real festive sacrilege. Christmas and its chief agent—Santa Claus.

Who is this overweight, conspicuously costumed, nocturnal, breaking-and-entering alien with no visible means of support? Does he collect GST on all the gifts he leaves? Does he declare to Revenue Canada all the milk and cookies he scarfs? Are the elves getting time and a half? Does the SPCA know about the work burden those reindeer face? Does he have a licence for that off-road vehicle, which, by the way, appears to have no running lights for night travel . . .

I'd like to put these questions to the infamous Mister Claus. Preferably in a court of law. The Supreme Court, even. Provided we could have the Chief Justice dress up as Ronald McDonald and the court officers all wearing Barney costumes.

I mean . . . we wouldn't want to frighten the children, would we?

Cool-as-a-Cucumber Cal

You know what this country needs, my friends? What this country needs is (I can't believe I'm saying this) another politician.

And an American politician at that.

Not just any American politician, mind. What this country could really use is the man who served as the thirtieth president of the United States of America, Calvin Coolidge. A pale, skinny Republican with red hair, freckles, a bony nose, a down-turned mouth that seldom turned up, and a pair of legs that almost certainly never did the Charleston.

As a warm and caring human being, Cool Cal fell somewhat short of, say, Alan Alda. Alice Roosevelt Longworth sniffed that Coolidge had been weaned on a pickle. His own wife claimed that he won her hand over other potential suitors only because "he outsat everybody else." Coolidge played his entire life like a bad poker hand, which is to say, close to the vest and stingily.

Most of all—and here's the blessed part about Calvin Coolidge—most of all, he hardly ever said a word. Well, he had a voice that quavered like a badly tuned A string on an open-fret banjo, but that's not the reason he bit his tongue. Coolidge didn't talk much because he knew it was smarter not to. "If you don't say anything, you won't be called on to repeat it," he once snapped—and for Cool Cal that was a filibuster.

His office efficiency amazed onlookers. Coolidge was able to see a near endless daisy chain of visitors and supplicants every day, but invariably finished his work at 5:00 p.m. A visiting governor moaned, "I'm at my desk every night until nine o'clock—what's the difference?" Coolidge looked at the governor and replied, "You talk back."

Coolidge got such a reputation as a zipperlip that it became a high-level Washington parlour game to get him to open up. One Washington socialite, famous for her beguiling ways, manoeuvred herself next to the president at a dinner and purred in his ear, "Mister Coolidge, I've made a bet that I can get more than two words out of you."

Cal swivelled in his seat and fixed the woman with a pair of iguana eyes. His lips parted . . . the voice croaked, "You lose."

But the man was not without humour and his spartan linguistics enhanced the effect. As in the time he and Mrs. Coolidge toured a government farm. When they came to the chicken pens, Mrs. Coolidge was quite taken with the rooster and inquired as to how many times he, um, you know, serviced the hens.

"Oh, dozens of times a day, ma'am," answered the tour guide.

"Tell that to the president," said Mrs. Coolidge.

The president came along and looked at the rooster. Informed of the animal's prowess, he asked, "Same hen every time?"

"Oh, no. Different hen each time, sir," said the guide.

"Tell that to Mrs. Coolidge," said Cal.

Good line, but I doubt that Cal was much fun in the sack. As Dorothy Parker said when informed that Coolidge had died, "How can they tell?"

Nope, Calvin Coolidge was probably a dud as a stud and certainly a disaster as a political leader.

But he was quiet about it. We've had a succession of disastrous politicians, randy and otherwise. I'd settle for quiet, wouldn't you?

The Hockey Stick Forever

S ome countries have it easy when it comes to national symbols. The
Yanks have the bald eagle. England has the bulldog. Scotland and
Ireland have the thistle and shamrock, respectively.

It's not so simple for Canada. The Maple Leaf? It's fine for
folks in southern Ontario but it's politically incorrect among the
Québécois, and it's a bit of an anomaly on the Prairies, not to mention much of the Maritimes and the great, largely bald rock called
Newfoundland.

As for Canadians in the Far North—they seldom see a tree,
much less a maple.

Some Canadian communities come up with their own symbols.
Sudbury has a giant nickel on its doorstep. The town of Wawa has a
fibreglass goose and on the outskirts of Kenora, Ontario, you'll find
a humungous muskellunge leaping into the northwestern Ontario
skies.

Oh yes, and Toronto has the concrete stalagmite called the
CN Tower and Vegreville, Alberta, basks in the shadow of a huge
Ukrainian Easter Egg—and these icons are all fine and dandy
but . . .

They miss the point, I think. They don't symbolize Canada for
ALL Canadians.

There's only one symbol that can truly do that and you'll find it at the town limits of Duncan, British Columbia.

It's a giant hockey stick.

Well, sure. What could be more Canadian? Is it possible that there's a single citizen in this country who wouldn't recognize—*instantly*—a hockey stick?

You don't have to don the skates to be savvy about the lumber. You don't even have to play the game to use one. I haven't hunkered down over a face-off circle in twenty years, but hockey sticks are an important part of my life.

Especially broken ones.

I use them to hold up my tomato plants each summer and to mark the ends of my garden rows. I have also pressed a sawed-off Sherwood Shur-shot into service when a strut in my hammock collapsed a few summers back. Works like a charm.

I've used hockey sticks to scrape snow off my windshield and to "slap-shoot" frozen "calling cards" from the next-door neighbour's German shepherd into aforesaid neighbour's backyard.

Sorry about the one that landed on your barbecue, Fred.

I've always considered myself pretty creative when it comes to finding uses for hockey sticks, but I am a mere babe in the arena compared to Doctor Floydd Mackenzie.

Floydd (yes, there are two ds) is a denizen of Red Deer, Alberta, and the author of a book called *One Hundred and One Ways To Recycle a Hockey Stick,* published by Red Deer College Press. Floydd really has come up with 101 ways to use your basic hockey stick—everything from reaming out eaves troughs to serving as a tiller on a sailboat.

Doctor Mackenzie's book (lavishly illustrated) shows hockey sticks used as fishing rods, leg splints, even emergency kayak paddles (although the kayak does have a tendency to "hook").

Doctor Mackenzie claims that his research has taken him around the globe, chasing down Canada's most famous symbol. He says he's found hockey sticks serving as bootracks in North Dakota, ceiling fan blades in Maine, and tribal masks in the jungles of New Guinea.

The most exotic example of hockey stick recycling in Doctor

Mackenzie's book? Well, my favourite among the 101 cited is an easy chair made from two goal sticks and four regular sticks and a welter of meticulously braided hockey tape which the author swears he discovered on a front porch in Stündeskanbe, Sweden.

And I believe him.

Of course, I'm biased.

My wife's relatives all hail from Ürepullenmilaig, Norway.

The Importance of the Arts

The first people of Canada attached a lot more importance to names than we do. In the old days, back before we took away their land and rewarded them with a lifetime supply of Bibles, Indians thought long and hard about what they would call their children. They wanted the name to reflect the personality. Thus, it could be months—in some cases, years—before an Indian assumed his given name. Look at the hero in that big Hollywood hit movie of a few years back. He was a middle-aged US cavalryman before the Indians finally got around to naming him "Dances with Wolves."

Well, what's good enough for Kevin Costner is good enough for me. I want a name change.

And I'm not fussy. You can call me "Fumbles with Keyboard" or "Snores in Church" or "He Who Walks About with Fly Unzipped." I don't care what you call me.

As long as it isn't Arthur.

I'm sick of Arthur. I've been lugging it around for more than half a century now, and I never much liked it.

Mind you, I hated it even more when I was a kid. Back then I was "Artie."

It is extremely difficult to establish one's status as a major teenage sex symbol when the family telephone rings, and your sister answers it, then yells, "Artie, some girl wants to talk to you!"

It got worse. Later, I spent a couple of years in England and heard how plummy, upper-class Brits attacked my moniker.

"Awwwwthuh," they called me. Sounded vaguely like a sea lion with indigestion.

Could be worse. At least my parents didn't name me Attila. Or Adolph. Or Oswald, Lee, or Harvey.

Names are fickle. Very few American parents are naming their children George these days. Just as on this side of the border, new-born males sporting the name of Brian are noticeably scarce.

"Arthur" doesn't carry such a tattered pedigree. *Au contraire.* There's Artie Shaw and Artur Schopenhauer and Arturo Toscanini.

Not to mention loveable old King Arthur.

And then, of course, there's our great moment of glory in Wardsville, Ontario. True story. Back in the summer of 1983, a government bureaucrat—the assistant deputy minister in the Ontario Ministry of Citizenship and Culture—wrote a letter to all the municipal clerks in the province. Purpose: to ask each clerk to "submit a short brief or letter concerning the Arts in their municipality—how they are regarded, how they are funded, what effect they have on the life or the economy of the municipality . . ."

This is one letter he got back:

> Dear Sir
>
> Reference your letter dated 10 August 1983 requesting information on the Arts in our municipality.
>
> We are pleased to advise that we have four.
>
> Art Harold
> Art Morgan
> Art Marks
> Art Sweet
>
> They are extremely well regarded in the community. They are mostly funded by Old Age Security Pension and

Canada Pension, and all contribute to the economy in their day-to-day living.

We are pleased that you are interested in our Arts. However, we have many other names that also deserve recognition, such as William, Charles, Henry, etc., particularly many of the feminine gender, Mary, Helene, Ellen, etc. We would be pleased to forward you a full list if you so wish.

Yours truly,
Harold Turton
Clerk,
Village of Wardsville

There's my answer. I don't have to change my name. I'll just move to Wardsville, where the Arts are really appreciated.

Black Tie and Tales

1999

Murphy's Law

One thing you've got to say for fame: it's certainly democratic. No age restrictions. No race, gender, or political qualifiers. Fame can happen in a heartbeat. It did for Edward A. Murphy, Jr. One moment, Ed was a run-of-the-mill US air force engineer, plugging away at some obscure rocket-sled experiments.

Next moment, he was a household name.

See—way back in 1949, some technician designed sixteen doohickeys to be used in one of Ed Murphy's experiments. Now, there were two ways these doohickeys could be glued in place: a right way and a wrong way. The technician had methodically installed all sixteen the wrong way.

And that's when Edward A. Murphy, Jr. is thought to have shaken his head and said, "You know, if anything can go wrong, it will."

And Edward A. Murphy, Jr. might just as well have hung up his lab smock right there, because with those words he ascended to the pantheon of immortality.

He had unknowingly promulgated Murphy's Law. And what a cottage industry that spawned. Now we have not only Murphy's Law, but also Murphy's Corollaries, Murphy's Faux Pas, and a whole mongrel mix of Murphy maxims for virtually every human misadventure.

Murphy's Corollary Number One states that Murphy's Law may be delayed or suspended for an indefinite period of time, provided that such delay or suspension will result in a greater catastrophe at a later date.

Murphy's Computer Law: No matter how good a deal you get on computer components, the price will always drop immediately after your purchase.

Murphy's Law of Social Behaviour: Light-coloured clothing attracts dark-coloured food spills; dark-coloured clothing attracts light-coloured food spills.

Murphy's Law of Food Preparation: Ovens either overcook or undercook—with the exception of microwave ovens, which always overcook *and* undercook at the same time.

Murphy's Law of Vending Machines: There are only two times when vending machine operators appear: when you kick the machine in disgust, and when you try to wrestle it into giving back your money.

Teachers have their own Murphy's Law. It says that when a teacher is late, the teacher will meet the principal in the hall. If the teacher is late and does not meet the principal, the teacher is late for a faculty meeting.

There are Murphy's laws for musicians, Murphy's laws for dances, Murphy's laws for—there's a Murphy's Law for everything—up to and including love and war.

Murphy's Law of Combat: The only thing more accurate than incoming enemy fire is incoming friendly fire.

And of course the Murphy Combat Law Corollary: Friendly fire . . . isn't.

As for love—well, the original Murphy's Law pretty well covers that, but there are some valuable Murphy addendums. Murphy's Law of Mate Selection: All the good ones are taken. Corollary: If the person isn't taken, there's a good reason.

Murphy's Laws. I don't know whether Edward A. Murphy, Jr. is laughing or crying over his law. You see, Murphy never said Murphy's Law. What Murphy said was: "If there are two or more ways to do something, and one of those ways can result in a catastrophe, then someone will do it." Unquote.

Which is not quite the same as saying, "Anything that can go wrong, will."

Therein lies the ultimate irony about Edward A. Murphy, Jr. He's world-famous for saying something he never said.

But then, that's just Murphy's Law at work, right?

Larking About

The French poet Paul Valery once said a pretty smart thing on the subject of looking at things. I mean *really* looking at things. "To look," said Valery, "is to forget the names of the things you are seeing."

I think I know what he means. I used to hike with a biologist pal until I couldn't stand it any more. We'd be walking along and maybe a big red-tailed hawk would swoop across the sky. "Wow, did you see that?" I'd babble.

"*Buteo jamaicensis*" my biologist would murmur smugly. "Immature male."

He was always like that. He never saw that Lily Tomlin thing that rabbits do with their mouths, or the Picassoesque dance of a monarch butterfly across a meadow, or the saucy "up yours" semaphore of a disappearing white-tailed rump. He saw *Danaus plexippus* and *Odocoileus virginianus*. Which are the correct terms for a monarch and a white-tailed deer—all very true and scientifically accurate, but . . . kind of unfulfilling.

It's perplexing for me, because as a writer, I want to know the names of things.

Which is where one of my favourite books comes in. It's a skinny one, called *An Exaltation of Larks*. The author, James Lipton, has brought together some of the wonderful collective terms the English language has for things like . . . well, like a gaggle of geese, a school of fish, a pride of lions, a flock of sheep.

Lesser-known, almost-forgotten terms too. Like a leap of leopards, a sounder of swine, a rafter of turkeys, and a kindle of kittens.

And some terms so beautiful, so apt, it's hard to imagine how we ever let them slip out of usage. How about a murmuration of starlings?

A bouquet of pheasants? A knot of toads? A hover of trout? A peep of chickens? And perhaps best of all, the title of the book—an exaltation of larks?

James Lipton is still alive, and still collecting collectives. Inventing them too. He's got a new book out, *An Exaltation of Business and Finance*. (I know . . . it doesn't exactly sing, does it?) But I think Lipton wrote Exaltation Two with tongue firmly lodged in buccal cavity. He's having a lot of fun collectivizing the business world of the late twentieth century.

His collective term for a group of accountants? Why, a column, of course. Similarly, he gives us a riddle of economists, a flush of plumbers, a drove of cabbies, a slouch of models, a pound of pianists, and a lot of realtors.

Not to mention a nucleus of physicists, a rash of dermatologists, and—in recognition of all those casting couches in Hollywood—a pinch of producers.

Lipton carries on a game that English speakers have been playing with the language for at least 600 years. It's a game anyone can play with any degree of bite. Lipton also offers an odium of politicians, an unction of undertakers, a glaze of tourists, a grope of groupies, and a shrivel of critics.

Well, no shrivels from this critic. Make it a bushel basket of thank-yous to James Lipton for reminding us what fun our language can be. And always has been.

An Exaltation of Larks. Try it. It's, well, a barrel of laughs.

Joking Newfies

Canada's thirteenth prime minister, John George Diefenbaker, probably had the healthiest attitude toward public-opinion polls. Back in the early 1960s a reporter asked the Chief what he thought of a newspaper poll that showed his popularity was on the wane.

Diefenbaker, eyes blazing, looked down at the reporter and thundered, "Poles? Poles? You know what dogs do to poles!"

And fair comment too. The trouble with polls is that they are mostly wrong, irrelevant—or they tell you things that anyone with the IQ of a cauliflower already knows.

Take this recent *Maclean's* magazine poll. "Newfoundlanders Are Canada's Busiest Lovers," it shrieks.

Yeah . . . so?

Is this supposed to be a surprise? The pollsters thought perhaps that retirees in Victoria or brokers on Bay Street could seriously challenge residents of the Rock when it comes to *amour*?

I thought everybody knew that Newfoundland was the love nest of the Canadian psyche. I mean, look at the place names!

Take a short drive up the east coast of Trinity Bay, and before you can say I'se the Bye you'll find yourself passing through a trio of hamlets called Heart's Delight, Heart's Desire, and Heart's Content.

Toronto has the Frederick G. Gardiner Expressway. Newfoundland has Tickle Cove.

British Columbia has Richmond and Comox and Surrey.

Newfoundland has Bareneed and Ha Ha Bay and Nancy Oh.

And that's without even getting into the lascivious Newfoundland place names—names like Cupids and Spoon Cove. Leading Tickles and Conception Bay. Comfort Cove. Breakheart Point. Happy Valley.

Goose Bay. Not to mention Dildo, Dildo Arm, Dildo Cove, Dildo Islands, Dildo Pond, Dildo Run, and South Dildo.

And, of course, Come by Chance.

Pretty hard to be a puritan when you're living in a suggestible landscape like that.

Some Newfoundlanders claim it's the seafood diet that gives them their sexual stamina. Others say it's the combination of isolation and even tougher than usual economic times that account for the popularity of mankind's oldest indoor sport.

I think it might be something else.

Anyone who's ever visited Newfoundland cannot fail to notice that the residents there still cling to something that the rest of us seem to have misplaced.

I don't know what to call it. It seems to be made up of generous dollops of innocence, genuine friendliness, innate kindness, and an unsinkable urge to enjoy life. Which they do, in spite of a grim climate, an unforgiving ocean, a moribund economy—and the stupid Newfie jokes the (secretly envious) rest of Canada tells about them.

You want a Newfie joke? I'll tell you one. I heard it in a bar on Duckworth Street one night when a raucous table of "Come from Aways" was filling the smoky air with Newfie jokes.

It went on for a while until finally the waiter, a brawny Bayman, came over to the table, put down his tray, and leaned on our table on his two hairy fists.

It looked like trouble. Until he opened his mouth.

"There was a Toronto feller came here to live in Sin Jahn's t'ree years ago," he told us. "After a couple of months he noticed a strange t'ing while he was shavin' one morning. He had this brown ring runnin' right across his forehead. Well, sir, he rushed right down to the emergency ward of the hospital. The doctor examined the ring on his forehead. Didn't say a word. The feller wit' the ring said, 'What is it, Doctor? Is it serious?' The doctor looked at him and said, 'You're from Toronto, are ye?'

"'That's right!' said the feller wit' the ring. 'But how could you know that? And what is this brown ring, anyway?'

"''Tis nothing to worry about,' said the doctor. 'You're merely full of shit and down a quart.'"

And then the waiter bought us a round of beer.

English as a Second Language

Back in the eighteenth century there was an Englishman by the name of Benjamin Schulze who could recite the Lord's Prayer in 215 languages. A certain Cardinal Mezzofante of Bologna was apparently fluent in "some fifty or sixty" tongues. Mr. Berlitz—the guy who invented the Berlitz method—claimed fluency in fifty-eight languages . . . and Sir John Bowring, one-time governor of Hong Kong, claimed to speak one hundred languages and to read one hundred more.

Even the American wit Dorothy Parker had a lady friend whom she said "speaks eighteen languages and can't say 'no' in any of them."

My question is, with all these lingomeisters around—how do you account for foreign-language movie subtitles? You know—the line of English translation that runs along the bottom of the screen while Bruce Lee or Toshiro Mufine is rattling away in Chinese or Japanese? They don't always quite . . . capture the nuances, do they?

Here's a few collectible English subtitles culled from films made in Hong Kong over the past few years:

"You daring, lousy guy!"

And another one, shouted by a policeman at a crook who's barricaded himself in a house: "I'll fire aimlessly if you don't come out!"

There's a Chinese movie where the hero is about to be executed by a firing squad. His last words? "I am damn unsatisfied to be killed in this way."

And my favourite. The muscle guy from the Triad looks at the hero and growls menacingly: "Take my advice or I'll spank you without pants!"

Ah, well, there was a fine old tradition of mutilating cinema English long before the Easterners gave us their two-yen worth. The movie mogul Sam Goldwyn was legendary for twisting simple speech into hilarious linguistic pretzels at the drop of a misplaced metaphor. He repeatedly referred to Joel McCrea, one of the stars in his stable, as Joe McRail. And once Goldwyn showed off the latest addition to his art collection—a canvas he introduced proudly as "my favourite Toujours Lautrec."

Sam was not a linguist. He had enough trouble handling English. Once he toyed with the idea of buying the rights to a novel that dealt with alternative sexuality—not what you'd call commercially viable subject matter in Hollywood of the 1940s and 1950s. A studio adviser whispered in his ear, "Sir, we can't film that. It's about lesbians."

"All right," said Goldwyn, "where they got lesbians, we'll use Austrians."

But the Naugahyde mantle for garbled cinematic English must, I think, go to the film director Michael Curtiz. Curtiz directed many movies, including the classic *Casablanca*. Curtiz—a.k.a. the Mad Hungarian—had a wonderful sense of mastery on the movie set, but less when it came to the English tongue. It was Curtiz who, during the filming of *The Charge of the Light Brigade,* attempted to initiate the stampede of hundreds of riderless horses past the cameras by booming through his megaphone "Hokay, now . . . brrang on de ampty horses!"

The entire set collapsed in laughter, which sent the Hungarian-born Curtiz into a towering rage. "YOU AND YOUR STINKING EENGLISH LANGUAGE!" he boomed through the megaphone, "YOU THEENK I KNOW BUGGER NOTHING. BUT I AM TELLING YOU, I KNOW BUGGER ALL!"

Canada: Feel the Diffidence!

Americans with highest glee
Applaud the climber of the tree
Englishmen have half a mind
The tree is not the proper kind
Canadians with tiny frown
Take an axe and chop it down.

—ROBIN SKELTON

O Canada. It's true, you know—this country does drag a huge psychic sea anchor behind it, slowing down its passage through the international shipping lanes. Canadians are diffident, cautious—second-guessers by nature.

Americans say, "Hell, let's go for it!"

Canadians say, "But what will the neighbours think?"

Canadianism has its good side. We don't run roughshod over other national sensibilities. It will be a long time before Canadian troops invade Grenada, subvert the government of Chile, or bomb Iraq. It's not our style.

But there's a downside too. There's a draggy side effect to being Canadian. Don't take my word for it. Ask the Kinsmans.

Bob and Rita Kinsman own a very successful motel/restaurant

complex in cottage country—the Muskoka district of Ontario. The Blue Heron Restaurant and Motel has seven rental units, a twenty-three-seat restaurant, a lakeside dock, and a one-bedroom apartment.

A success story—with just one tiny blackfly in the ointment. The Kinsmans were approaching retirement age. They wanted to get out of the grind and enjoy themselves.

And they hit on a novel way to do that. Bob and Rita Kinsman announced that they were sponsoring a competition. Contestants had to first pony up a hundred dollars each. Then they had to write a 200-word essay explaining why they would like to take over the Blue Heron Restaurant and Motel. After all the entries were in, judges supplied by the South Muskoka Literacy Society would go over the essays and choose the grand-prize winner.

In other words, for a hundred bucks and a couple of cents worth of ballpoint ink, somebody was going to win a flourishing resort business, worth close to half a million bucks.

The Kinsmans are an adventurous couple, but they're not flat out crazy. They reserved the right to cancel the contest and refund the money if they got fewer than 4,000 entries.

It became a media sensation. The newspaper wire services picked up the story. TV crews showed up to film the Kinsmans and shoot a little footage of the sun going down from the Blue Heron dock.

The story got so much airplay that even the bureaucrats in Ottawa got wind of it.

And they proceeded to do what bureaucrats do best: they killed it stone dead.

Ottawa announced that because of the minimum entry requirement, the contest was illegal.

"The police said we could appeal," noted Rita Kinsman ruefully. "But it would have to be to the Supreme Court of Canada, and that could easily cost $100,000."

So the contest is dead. The 300 entrants who have written their essays and paid their entry fee will get their money back, and the Kinsmans will try to sell their business the conventional, Canadian way. Through a real-estate agent on the open market.

Pity. A pity that a little grassroots initiative gets stomped to death by the bean-counters in Ottawa. Reminds me of the story Derek Burney, Canada's ambassador to the US, used to tell about the Newfoundland fisherman carrying a pail of lobsters up from the wharf. A passer-by warned him that the lobsters could get away because there was no lid on the pail.

"Not to worry, bye," says the fisherman. "These are Canadian lobsters. Soon as one makes it to the top, the others will drag him down."

Black Like Yours Truly

In America, only the successful writer is important.
In France, all writers are important. In England, no
writer is important. In Australia, you have to explain
what a writer is.

—GEOFFREY COTTERELL

And in Canada? What of the Great White Frozen Attic? What's it like to be a professional writer in Canada?

Well, as a scribbler who's kept the bailiffs at bay for thirty-odd years by wielding nothing more lethal than a single-action Olivetti, I'd have to say Canadian writers fall somewhere between the American and Australian extremes. Which is to say that successful writers (Margaret Atwood, Robertson Davies, Alice Munro, Mordecai Richler) don't exactly have to take in laundry to make ends meet. On the other hand, they can still pilot their own grocery cart down at the local supermarket without worrying about being mobbed by groupies in the frozen-food section.

People have a lot of misconceptions about the writing business. The biggest delusion is that writing for a living will make you rich. Not likely. If you envision a life of wallowing in megabucks in the

166

back seat of a chauffeur-driven stretch limo, best you try some other line of work—like mugging or high seas piracy or criminal law. Most writers in Canada are lucky to keep their noses above the poverty line.

Another major misconception about writing is that it is somehow easy, romantic, and fun. It is to whimper ruefully. There's nothing fun or romantic about sitting down in front of a blank piece of paper or a vacant computer screen day after day. And easy? It looks that way only when it's done well.

If you ever want to have your nose rearranged without benefit of plastic surgery, get yourself introduced to a writer and say, "Yeah, but what do you *really* do for a living?"

A brain surgeon once cornered Margaret Laurence at a literary cocktail party and trumpeted, "So you're an author! That's great! You know, when I retire from medicine, I'm going to be an author!"

Margaret Laurence looked at him through those hooded eyes, took a drag on her ever-present cigarette, and replied softly: "Fascinating. And when I retire, I plan to take up brain surgery."

Now, don't misunderstand me—I don't want to make writing sound like the root canal of career choices. It's not. The only real dangers in this line of work are nasty critics, unreasonable editors, and the odd paper cut.

Oh, yes . . . and there is the ego problem.

It doesn't happen often, but once in a while your typical Canadian author will become somewhat . . . full of himself. Put on airs. Act like he or she is actually important.

Happened to me not long ago. I'd just published my fifth book and decided that, dammit, real writers don't go around in T-shirts, jeans, and baseball caps. Chap in my position ought to look more . . . well, *authorly.* So I went out and bought a tweed jacket, complete with side vents and suede elbow patches.

I felt like Pierre Berton by way of Robertson Davies with a touch of Farley Mowat in my new threads. On an impulse, I sashayed into a bookstore, briskly rapped the bell, and asked the startled clerk if they carried "that new book by Black."

"Who?" the clerk asked blankly.

"Black. Arthur Black. Clever fellow. Probably in your Canadiana section. Or perhaps under World Humour . . ."

The clerk had never heard of him (me). And neither had his computer.

"This is intolerable!" I blustered. "The man has written five books. Surely a bookstore this large would have at least one of them!"

The clerk searched and searched. And finally, deep in the second-hand racks, just beside the remainders bin, he came up with one dog-eared, bookworm-riddled copy of my first book, *Basic Black.*

My book had been filed, along with books by Dick Gregory, H. Rap Brown, a biography of Mohammed Ali, and the collected speeches of Martin Luther King, under Black Revolutionary Studies.

Please Marry Me (This Is a Recording)

This morning I find myself pondering the predicament (I'm pretty sure it's a predicament) of one Vernon Pierce. Mr. Pierce is a thirty-three-year-old resident of Glendale, Arizona. Pretty good-looking guy—an ex-model, as a matter of fact. Pretty attractive to the ladies too, apparently. At least his wives think so. Yeah, *wives*. Four of them. At once.

That's right. Old sly fox Vernon is currently married to four different women. He also has a few girlfriends, but that's just on the side. How does he do it? Well, his little black book helps. Vernon's book doesn't contain addresses. It contains details of what he's told, and to whom, so he can keep his stories straight. Police also found a small card in his wallet labelled Who to Marry. Clearly, Vernon wasn't finished yet. At least he wasn't until Wife #3—or possibly #2—sent the cops to check up on him, and they found themselves knocking on Vernon's door alongside Wife #1. Or maybe it was #4. Vernon's now in the Glendale slammer, doing time for bigamy and fraud. And if he's having conjugal relations, it's probably not with anyone he'd care to make Wife #5.

Still, four wives at once . . . seems a fairly daunting prospect from this vantage point. Not a patch on Tommy Manville, of course. Tommy was the heir to the Johns-Manville fortune, and he spent most of it on wives. He was a serial bridegroom, unlike Vernon. Tommy got married eleven times and divorced ten, each divorce costing him pailfuls of money. Or as Tommy put it, almost poetically, "She cried, and the judge wiped her tears with my chequebook."

And Tommy looks like a wallflower next to the most married man in *The Guinness Book of Records.* That honour goes to Glynn Scotty Wolfe, who got himself hitched to twenty-seven different women.

One after the other. Oh, and that would be *Reverend* Wolfe, by the way. He was a Baptist minister in—oh, well, now it figures—Blythe, *California.*

Ah, but I've been saving the best for last. The most married man—biggest bigamist, if you will—in the monogamous world would have to be Giovanni Vigliotto. Or Nikolai Peruskov. Or perhaps Fred Jepp.

Giovanni, Nikolai, Fred. Those were all names used by one man who got married—are you ready?—104 times. He tied the knot in twenty-seven different US states and fourteen foreign countries. In 1968 he married four different women on one ocean cruise.

Nobody knows where Giovanni or Nikolai or Fred was born, but the experts agree he died in 1991, serving time, like Vernon—remember Vernon?—for fraud and bigamy.

And here's a still-healthy Vernon Pierce with a measly four wives and a half-dozen or so girlfriends, crying the blues about how hard done by he is. "It wasn't always fun," whines Vernon. "Guys fantasize about something like this, but you don't have your own life."

Oh, yeah, Vernon? Breaking our hearts. Go tell it to Giovanni. Or Nikolai. Or Fred.

Dear Innkeeper

You stay in hotels much? I do. More than I'd like to, actually. Sleeping in strange beds under rented sheets with the meter running, as it were, is an odd way to spend one's time when you think about it. Do it too much and it can lead to the development of certain idiosyncrasies.

Take Vicki Gabereau. She says the first thing she does when she gets into a new hotel room is turn on the TV. That's the second thing I do.

The first thing I do is steal the matches.

It's true. I run all around the hotel room gathering up the matchbooks and stuffing them in my suitcase. I don't even smoke. I don't have a fireplace at home. Or any oil lamps. I light maybe half a dozen candles a year, tops. So why do I steal the matches? I have no idea. I control more matchsticks than E.B. Eddy. I own more sulphur than Satan. I can't solve your marital problems or work out your income tax for you, but if you ever need a light, I'm your man.

I don't just spend my hotel time commandeering matchbooks, though. I spend a fair amount of time thinking about what's good about hotel rooms.

And what's not so good.

What's not so good are: windows that don't open, camouflaged thermostats that only James Bond could find, minuscule bath towels, chambermaids who drumknuckle your door at dawn and carol, "ROOOOOOOOOM check!" and radios that never pick up CBC. Why is it that hotel radios never pick up CBC? Is it a Ted Rogers plot? I can get all the country and western, evangelical, "Sex with Sue" hotline, and late-night phone-in shows a body could never ask for . . . but I can never pick up CBC.

Here's another observation—Conrad Hilton, if you're listening—lose the complimentary shoe mitt. For one thing, most people are wearing Adidas or Nikes or Sauconys these days. And for another thing, the shoe mitts don't even work very well. Ever tried to shine your shoes with one, Conrad? I thought not. Deep-six the shoe mitt.

And while you're at it, why not transform the hotel rooms that are over the disco or next to the ice machine? Why not turn them into towel-storage rooms or something? Nobody wants to try to sleep while LaToya Jackson is whooping and yodelling—or while the ice machine is going BODODODODODODODODOOOD-LUMP every twenty minutes. And no hotel guest will ever ever forgive you for sentencing them to those rooms from hell.

And one more suggestion, O, hoteliers and innkeepers of the world. And this one doesn't come from me. It comes from Joseph Brodsky, a Nobel laureate and Poet Laureate of the US of A. Mr. Brodsky died a few years go, but not before he laid his head on more than a few hotel pillows. He knows the sterility of your average hotel room. And he has a solution.

Joseph Brodsky and a friend, Andrew Carroll, conspired to stock hotel rooms with . . . poetry books.

Yes! Anthologies of Emily Dickinson, Walt Whitman, and Robert Frost. Already hotel chains in Massachusetts, Virginia, and Texas have agreed to lay in free books of poetry right alongside the sappy shopping brochures and the chirpy "How're We Doin'?" evaluation questionnaires. The rationale? As Brodsky put it, "When poetry is available you can make a choice between a drug and a book, a gun and a book—God knows what."

Free poetry in the privacy of your hotel room. Sounds like a good deal to me. And God knows Canada has the raw material. Leonard Cohen, Margaret Atwood, Irving Layton, Earle Birney.

I wouldn't be averse to finding Susan Musgrave nestled next to my Gideon the next time I check into a hotel room.

Tell ya what, you hotel keepers, I'll cut you a deal. Give me a little free poetry in my room and I promise to stop stealing your matches.

Taking It All Off

The nude thing. Let me try to tell you what it's like to sit bare-butted on a log on a beach talking to a woman you've just met who also just happens to be naked as a jay bird.

Easy. It felt easy.

There was Judy Williams, chairman of the Wreck Beach Preservation Society, and there was I . . . on Wreck Beach, a stretch of sand about twenty, twenty-five minutes from downtown Vancouver that just happens to be "clothing optional." Flesh to the left of us, flesh to the right of us. Acres and acres of burnished human flesh basting in the sun.

I don't come to such a situation easily, you know. Mine was a conventional, rural, southern Ontario, Louis St. Laurent-era upbringing, which is to say restrained . . . muffled . . . thwarted like a Japanese bonsai.

Were we taught that sex was dirty? No. We weren't taught that sex was anything. Sex was unimaginable. But bare flesh . . . *that* was pretty dirty.

I remember my Grade 8 teacher, Miss Sanford, wearing a slightly low-cut blouse one day. She leaned over to dump the shavings from the pencil sharpener in the wastebasket, betraying just a whisker of cleavage for no more than a millisecond.

Turned my knees to porridge.

I remember Mary Jane Chapman jogging doggedly around the high-school track one Thursday afternoon wearing those stupid baggy blue bloomers they made all the girls wear. Sad sacks that would make Sharon Stone look like a couch potato. My throat was so dry I couldn't swallow.

I lived through the age of the maxi, the midi, and the glory hallelujah mini skirt . . . watching that hem go up, up, way up . . . scarcely believing my luck at being alive and not blind.

No, I don't come lightly or nonchalantly to the sight of exposed female flesh. And yet . . . and yet. There I was, sitting naked on a log on Wreck Beach, talking to naked Judy Williams. And not blushing or giggling or ebbing or flowing. Feeling totally at ease.

As a matter of fact, it occurred to me that I felt even more at ease than if I'd been wearing a bathing suit. Because if I'd been wearing a bathing suit, I probably would have been conned into the old macho mug's game of trying to look fit. Sucking in my gut, puffing out my chest. When you're buck naked, surrounded by every conceivable variety of other naked people, there's no point in bluffing. People see what you are, so you might as well relax.

And I did. That was the greatest thing about being starkers on Wreck Beach. Aside from feeling the sun and the wind on parts of my body where I'd never felt the sun and wind before, I felt totally relaxed.

And yet . . . and yet . . .

Call me twisted. Call me an incorrigible old throwback to my uptight, priggish, and puritanical upbringing, but I have to confess that as Judy and I packed up after our talk and she turned to go up the path ahead of me, I couldn't stop my eyes from casting a furtive glance at her, couldn't stop my mind from muttering, "I wonder what she looks like with her clothes on?"

Flash Black

2002

The Wonderful Game of Bloopers

Late autumn is probably the toughest time of year for the dedicated non-sports fan. The football season is in full campaign, with the Grey Cup and the Vanier Cup just fading in the rear-view mirror and the never-ending "bowls" (Rose, Gator, Orange, Hula, et cetera) just over the horizon. The National Hockey League season is grinding through its interminable season—and tennis, golf, and car racing we have with us always.

You might infer, from the snide tone of the above, that I am not a major sports fan. Untrue. I am a passionate follower of a particular sector of the sports business that overlaps all venues.

The Play-by-Play Announcers Blooper Invitational.

I collect classic sportscaster boners—and there's a fruitful orchard in which to do my plucking.

My favourites? One spring, Larry Frattare broke into his broadcast coverage of a Pittsburgh Pirates game to lament the untimely death of the great black actor James Earl Jones. "I thought he was just tremendous in [the baseball film] *Field of Dreams*," Frattare intoned. "We're going to miss him."

Frattare's eulogy was premature. James Earl Jones was—and is—alive and well. The chap who died was the white racist James Earl Ray, the assassin of Martin Luther King.

Oh, well. All those James Earls look alike anyway.

Foot-in-mouth disease is not an affliction restricted to sports announcers south of the border. Frank Selke, Jr. once had his moment of truth in a between-periods interview with a young fan during a Canadiens-Rangers hockey game.

"Did you have a nice Christmas?" Selke asked the youngster.

"No."

"Why not?" Selke persisted. "I'm Jewish," the lad explained.

Curt Gowdy got into hot—or at least deep—water while broadcasting an AFL all-star game a few years back. The football field had been deluged with rain prior to the game, leaving huge puddles everywhere. "If there's a big pileup out there," observed Gowdy, "they'll have to give some players artificial insemination."

During a Yankees-Orioles game, the sports broadcaster Jerry Coleman interviewed the spouse of a famous baseball player about the hardships of being a baseball wife.

"When he's on the road, I have to take care of everything. I'm pretty much the man of the family," said the woman.

"Ah," said Coleman, "so you have to wear the pants in the family?"

"That's right," the wife agreed, "but when he comes home, I take them off."

And I'm sure Jim McKay of ABC's *Wide World of Sports* would like to have a second chance at covering the World Barrel Jumping Championships of 1986. "Leo Lebel has been competing with a pulled stomach muscle," McKay told TV watchers. "He's showing a lot of guts."

Then there was the fellow who was covering a PGA golf classic as Billy Casper approached the tee. "Billy, usually an expert putter, seems to be having difficulty with his long putts," he murmured into the microphone, adding thoughtfully, "however, he has no trouble dropping his shorts."

The sportscaster Chris Schenkel must still wince whenever he recalls a remark he made during a Honolulu football game. As the TV camera lingered on a particularly fetching blonde in the stands, Schenkel turned to his co-anchor, saying, "Bud, isn't that the young lady who gave us a lei before the game?"

My all-time favourite? I heard it on a live national football broadcast about fifteen years ago. The sportscaster, who shall remain mercifully nameless, was covering the last, dramatic seconds of the fourth quarter. His play-by-play went like this:

"He's fading back to pass ... He's going deep ... IT'S INTERCEPTED ON THE 30-YARD LINE! Mullins has the ball ... He's to the 40 ... crosses mid-field ... Now he's at the 50 ... the 40 ... He dodges a tackle ... He's running well ... to the 30 ... the 20 ... LOOKIT THAT SONOFABITCH RUN!"

It is perhaps unfair to hold sports announcers up to the same standards as, say, Lloyd Robertson or Peter Mansbridge. Sports commentators aren't hired for their knowledge of current events.

As Joe Theissman, football quarterback turned commentator, so eloquently put it: "Nobody in football should be called a genius. A genius is a guy like Norman Einstein."

Eh . . . What's Up, Doc?

Been down so long it looks like up to me.
—OLD BLUES LYRIC

I've got a question for you: Which way is "up"?

The question is not nearly as frivolous as it sounds. Why is it that we refer to Tuktoyaktuk as being "up north," but when we talk about Windsor, Ontario, we say it's "down south"?

For that matter, where do Calgarians get off referring to Torontonians as Easterners?

Not to a Haligonian they're not.

I remember the first time I became aware of the relativity of "up north." I was living in Toronto at the time, and I mentioned to an acquaintance that I was going "up north" for the weekend.

"Oh?" he said. "Whereabouts?"

"Barrie," I answered. He laughed till he cried.

He was from Sudbury.

Later, I moved to Thunder Bay, Ontario, and discovered that people from British Columbia still considered me an Easterner.

Easterner? In Thunder Bay, I was living in practically the dead centre of the whole danged country! If a Thunder Bay resident was an Easterner, what the hell was Joey Smallwood?

"Up" and "down," "east" and "west," "left" and "right"—they all mean different things to different people. I remember as a little kid squatting in my backyard and digging like a maniac with my tiny sand shovel. My dad came along when I was down about a foot and a half, smiled, and asked, "What do you think you're trying to do—dig a hole to China?"

I didn't know what he meant. So he explained to me that we all lived on this big ball called the earth, and if I dug deep enough and long enough, I would eventually tunnel right through to the other side of the ball—possibly in the middle of a street in downtown Beijing.

Cosmic stuff for a little kid to digest. What I couldn't get my mind around was the image of all these Chinese people walking around upside down on this giant ball we all shared.

Now I live on Canada's West Coast. That means that just about every day I wake up to radio newscasts and read newspaper stories about various happenings in "the Far East."

Which is to the left, or west, of where I live . . . if I think about it while I'm facing up, or north.

My Far East is St. John's, Newfoundland. Hong Kong is more like the Near West to me.

My grasp on reality is shaky enough without this complication. I find it all very confusing, and I personally hold Ptolemy responsible.

Ptolemy was an astronomer in ancient Egypt, about a century after the birth of Christ. It was Ptolemy who started the whole tradition of putting the North Pole at the tops of maps and globes—probably because the northern hemisphere was explored earlier than the rest of the globe, and those early cartographers just filled in the rest by adding to the bottom of their charts. Besides, it greatly simplified things when our notion of terrestrial geography was pictured on flat pieces of paper.

As the centuries passed, it became an unquestioned convention to place the North Pole at the top of the chart.

It became our geographical "up."

And that's just looking at it from the "earthly" point of view. Now that we're sending rockets to Mars, the moon, and Venus—

now that we fully acknowledge that planet Earth is but one whirling ball of dirt in a near-endless galaxy of whirling balls of dirt—the idea of "up" and "down," or even "left" and "right," becomes well-nigh ludicrous.

Everybody's "down" is somebody else's "up." Take the residents of Canada's southernmost city, Windsor, Ontario. You know what's immediately north of them?

The US city of Detroit.

You could look it up.

How Do You Spell Komik Relief?

Andrew Jackson, aside from being the seventh US president, was also a bad speller. Once, while trying to decide whether the word he wanted was *constitution* or *konstitushun*, Jackson threw down his quill pen and roared, "It's a damn poor mind that can think of only one way to spell a word!"

Jackson was right. Bad spelling is no indication of low intelligence. Look at Farley Mowat. The man writes like a dream, but he can't spell worth a damn. I know—in a previous incarnation as a sub-editor, I got to edit one of his manuscripts.

But for a fine writer like Mowat, there's no shortage of drones to take care of messy details like spelling and punctuation. Some poor spellers aren't so lucky. Take the tattooist who did a job on Joe Beahm.

Beahm had come into Body Art World, a tattoo joint in Asbury Park, New Jersey, with a special request: he wanted a tattoo on his back showing a knife stabbing into his shoulder blade. And under that, he wanted the words "Why not? Everybody else does."

"It was just something funny that I had in mind," says Beahm.

Funnier than he knew. When the blood dried and the tattoo was visible, the legend beneath the knife read, in letters a quarter of an inch high:

WHY NOT?
EVERYBODY ELESE DOES

Now Joe Beahm is bad-mouthing the tattooist, and the tattooist is suing Beahm for slander. Meanwhile, Joe Beahm is keeping his shirt on.

Spelling also turned out to be fairly critical in the streets of Hartford, Connecticut. Literally "in the streets." You know those road-painting contractors who get to stencil city streets with white lines, arrows, and instructions such as *No Left Turn* or *Quiet, Hospital Zone*? Well, there's one road-painting contractor in West Hartford who might be looking for a new line of work. He's the guy responsible for spraypainting, all over town, in three-foot-high letters:

SLOW DOWN
SCOHOL ZONE

Maybe I'm wrong—maybe the city will give him his road-painting job back, providing he signs up for a remedial spelling course at night school.

The late comedian Peter Sellers had a low tolerance for bad spellers. When he received a request for "a singed, autographed photograph," Sellers gleefully hauled out a lighter, burned the edges of an eight-by-ten glossy, and popped it in the mail.

Two weeks later, he got another letter from the fan, thanking him for the photograph but wondering if he could trouble him for another, as "the one you sent is signed all around the edge."

Then there's the story about the professor who was correcting an essay by a student who wrote about his holiday in Venezuela. The student kept writing the word "burrow" instead of "burro."

The professor corrected it once. Twice. Three times. Finally, in exasperation, he wrote in the margin, "My dear sir: It is quite apparent that you do not know your ass from a hole in the ground."

What's in a Name?

What's in a name? That which we call a rose
By any other word would smell as sweet.
—WILLIAM SHAKESPEARE

Well, there are roses and then there are roses, Bill. Take the Pantone Color Institute of New Jersey. Pantone comes up with names for paint colours, and they don't mess with simple minded concepts like red, blue, and yellow. Pantone creates concoctions like "terra firma" (brown), "vintage claret" (dark red), "angel wink pink" and "orange you happy."

Silly, you think? Not very. Last year, one paint company took all its off-white paint tins off the shelves and re-dubbed them "antique silk." Sales more than doubled.

Names are important. And not just for paint cans. Ask Dick Assman how important a name is.

Dick Assman used to be an unheralded gas jockey at a Petro-Canada station on the outskirts of Regina.

Then David Letterman discovered him. The inherent absurdity of Mr. Assman's name struck a resounding chord in the anal-retentive humour quadrant of Letterman's brain, and Dick Assman became a running gag on Letterman's show. Each week, dopey

Dave would relate some tidbit about Dick Assman, and the studio audience (whose humour threshold is even less demanding than Letterman's) would roar with approval.

Dick Assman was famous. The ultimate butt of the Letterman wit, as it were.

Letterman should get out more. There are lots of people around with funnier names than Dick Assman's—some of them already famous. Anybody remember the president of Zimbabwe, one Rev. Canaan Banana? How about the archbishop of Manila, Cardinal Sin?

I'm not making these up, you know.

Rock stars have foisted some memorable monikers on an unsuspecting public. ZZ Top and Iggy Pop, Sid Vicious and Johnny Rotten come to mind. Some pop icons have even extended their zaniness to the second generation. The British singer David Bowie crowned his son Zowie.

Zowie Bowie. There's a kid that'll need either a great sense of humour or a wicked right cross.

Frank Zappa named his kids Dweezil and Moon Unit. What was the guy smoking?

The sports world has always been a haven of wacky handles. Baseball gave us Thurman Munson. Hockey produced Sheldon Kanageiser. And does anybody remember the great quarterback Y.A. Tittle? His full name was Yelberton Abraham Tittle.

Some kids obviously had sadists for parents. There's a fisherman in Warsaw, New York, who answers (reluctantly) to the name Dennis Elbow. There's a farmer in Kentucky whose driver's licence identifies him as Henry Ford Carr and a society dame in Houston, Texas, whose real name is Ima Hogg.

If you live in Los Angeles, you can have your legal work taken care of by an attorney named Lake Trout (and yes, he has a brother named Brook).

As for magnificent rolling names, how about Humperdinck Fangboner? He's a lumber dealer in Sandusky, Ohio—married to Fanny Fangboner. And then there's the firewood salesman in Cambridge, Massachusetts, Mr. Vestibule.

Mr. Marmalade P. Vestibule.

The most outrageous name of all time? You'd have to go some distance to beat the son born to John Brook in New York in 1876, a centennial year. Mr. Brook, who loved attending performances at the John Hodge Opera House and manufactured gargling oil, also supported Samuel J. Tilden, who was running for the US presidency.

So naturally, Mr. Brook christened his son John Hodge Opera House Centennial Gargling Oil Samuel J. Tilden Ten Brook.

His friends called him Buck.

And Still More Wacky Words

A spelling reformer indicted
For fudge was before the court cicted.
The judge said, "Enough—
His candle we'll snough
And his sepulcher shall not be whicted."

—ANONYMOUS

Do you ever think what it must be like for a newcomer to Canada? I mean a *real* newcomer—someone from Sri Lanka or Hong Kong or Ulan Bator, who not only has never heard of k.d. lang or W. Gretzky but doesn't even speak English?

Can you imagine trying to learn English as a second language? How long would it take you to figure out what a sign like *No Through Street* means? How long would it take you just to figure out how to pronounce that second word? Is it *thruff*, as in "rough"? *Throff*, as in "trough"? *Throe*, as in "though"? *Thrup*, as in "hiccough"? Or is it *thraow*, as in "bough"?

No, as a matter of fact, it's *throo*, as in "through."

In the labyrinthine logic of English, we lie in a bed but lay an egg.

A song is sung, but a criminal is hanged. And we don't

pronounce the *p* in pneumonia, the *d* in Wednesday, or the entire middle of words like Worcester and Leicester.

Or, for that matter, the *gh* in "through."

Ch is pronounced one way in "character," another way in "charter." Same with the letter *g* in "general" and "gun."

I'm glad I was born into an English-speaking family—I don't think I ever could have learned it from a book.

Especially if the book contained Janus words.

Are you familiar with Janus? He was a god the Romans honoured a couple of thousand years ago. Janus was heaven's doorman as far as they were concerned, and when they built statues of him, the Romans gave Janus two faces: one facing front, the other astern.

That's where the concept of Janus words comes from. They, too, have two faces, or meanings—and they face 180 degrees away from each other.

Take the word "cleave," for example. A loving couple can cleave to one another, but an axe can also cleave a chunk of firewood. Thus, "cleave" means both to stick together and to split apart.

Go figure.

How about the word "sanction"? The government sanctions the use of seat belts in cars, but it also employs sanctions against Zimbabwe. So "sanction" means to endorse and/or condemn.

Huh?

Similarly, "fast" can mean speedy or immobile. You can run fast or be stuck fast in the mud. You can "dust" a crop in a field (pour crud on to it), or you can "dust" the living-room table (wipe crud off it).

The word "left" can be used to mean either departed or still remaining. (He left this morning. There's one cupcake left.)

"Overlook" can be taken to mean inspect or ignore; "buckle" can mean to wilt or to tie together.

Can someone please tell me how any mere human being can be expected to make sense of a language that features Janus words— words that can have exactly opposite interpretations?

Like the word "conservative." My dictionary says it comes from the word "conserve," meaning to preserve and protect (the countryside).

So how does that explain Ralph Klein?

Fifty-four Channels and Nothing On

Imagine what it would be like if TV actually was good. It would be the end of everything we know.
—MARVIN MINSKY

I'm a middle-aged guy, still several years away from my old-age pension. I'm relatively hale and hearty—still ride a bike, paddle a kayak, go for long hikes and brisk swims. I can dance (albeit awkwardly), climb ladders, shoot a few hoops in the driveway, and even, once in a while, stay up to the wee hours of the morning. And yet . . . and yet . . .

I am old. Incredibly old. I'm so old, I grew up in a house without a TV set.

Am I a member of the last generation able to say that? Probably. When I tell young kids of my boob-tubeless upbringing, they look at me like I'm a Neanderthal just recently released from a melting glacier.

It seems incredible, even to me. I now have two television sets in my home, and I'm hooked up to cable, which means I get CBC and CTV and Baton, not to mention NBC, CBS, ABC, CNN, TNN, Life, A&E, The Women's Network, and a host of channels I don't even know the call signs of. We live in, as videophiles never cease to crow, a 500-channel universe—an electronic beehive whose potential would make pioneers like Alexander Graham Bell and Thomas Edison drool with envy.

And I look at it all and say, "Big deal."

Because what do I get from this vast tele-universe? I get crummy music videos, lame sitcoms, numbing religious scam shows, endless sports, and most of all, a plague of commercials trying to sell me stuff I don't want, can't use, and couldn't afford anyway.

I'm developing a severe case of Schwarzenegger thumb from zapping through the channels on my remote trying to find something watchable.

Pity. If I lived in Juneau, Alaska, my search would be over. I'd simply click on channel 23 and tuck the remote under the sofa cushions forever.

In Juneau, channel 23 is the designated station for GCI Cable. What you get when you tune in is live, twenty-four-hour coverage of Gastineau Channel, the main waterway through the city. You can watch sunrises, sunsets, boats passing, seagulls squawking, kids fishing, seasons changing—everything that happens every day along the banks and upon the waters of Gastineau Channel.

Folks in Juneau call it the Channel channel. And they love it.

GCI Cable first started broadcasting live coverage of the waterway in 1993. Money was tight for programming, and it was all the company could afford. Now the soothing "program" has become so popular that GCI refuses to bump it for regular programming. "We get more positive feedback from this than from anything we've ever done," said GCI's marketing manager.

Doesn't surprise me. When I lived in Thunder Bay, Ontario, some years ago, the local cable station used to broadcast a video of a roaring fire burning in a fireplace. You could turn on your TV and watch the fire for hours as it waxed and waned, the flames crackling merrily in your living room.

And you never had to take out the ashes.

There's a lesson here for TV programmers. US national cable networks are discovering that some of their most popular programs are funerals and memorial services. Why? Because it's real life, not

TV confection. And nobody's trying to scare, shame, titillate, or infuriate the viewers. It's just life going on.

Without commercials.

The possibilities are endless—how about an aquarium channel? Round-the-clock coverage of angel fish, neon tetras, and kissing gouramis floating about their business? How about a train channel, with the camera locked on a railway switching yard?

Heck, the programmers already have a prototype in place. They've got the Weather Network, where you get to watch changing weather patterns twenty-four hours a day.

Of course, there's really nothing very new about that. We watched a weather channel back when I was a nipper—long before television came along.

But back then, we called it a window.

Where There's Smoke, There's Ire

Smoking is, as far as I'm concerned, the entire point of being an adult.

The American humorist Fran Leibowitz wrote that about a decade ago. I doubt that she would write it today—if only because non-smokers would immediately burn her at the stake.

On second thought, naw. Way too much air pollution. They'd probably just crucify her.

There was a time, not so very long ago, when lighting up a butt was considered attractive, even sexy. Bogey and Bacall, Crawford and Coward—everybody who was anybody smoked. We smoked in airplanes and buses, in doctor's waiting rooms and restaurants. Nobody asked if they could smoke when they came to your house. Of course they could smoke. That's why you had ashtrays all over the place.

Well, no more. Smoking is definitely no longer glamorous. Former president Bill Clinton has officially denounced it. Our own prime minister (while gleefully continuing to pocket the tax money charged on each package of cigarettes) has publicly allowed that "hit's a bad 'abit."

Joe Camel, a cartoon character invented by the makers of

Camel cigarettes, has turned out to be just about the worst idea a Madison Avenue hack ever had. "Uncle Joe" has become a lightning rod for the American anti-smoking movement—a symbol of everything non-smokers detest and deplore. As a half-page ad in a recent edition of the *New York Times* asked, "After all, who should tell kids about tobacco? Their parents . . . or Uncle Joe?"

We live in smoker-hostile times. Anybody addicted to the weed will find herself segregated in restaurants, ostracized at social gatherings, and frowned upon the instant she flicks her Bic.

The building I work in has been declared a smoke-free zone. Nicotine junkies have to hie themselves off to a depressing little "smoking room" on the second floor. Others stand around in clumps on the sidewalk, puffing, coughing, and avoiding the eyes of pink-lunged, self-righteous colleagues.

It could be worse. Recently, 6,000 employees of Motorola's two plants in Illinois received a memo informing them that they risk being fired if caught smoking on Motorola property—and that includes sitting *in their own cars* while in the company parking lot.

There's a town in California where it's illegal to smoke anywhere *outdoors*.

So how do I feel about the escalating smoker's war? Ambivalent, actually. I've been on both sides of this particular no man's land. I kicked a twenty-five-year habit, stayed clean for five years, then strayed again. As I write, I haven't smoked for three months, but I don't kid myself. I know I'm only one puff away from being a two-pack-a-day man.

I know that smoking is a grubby, expensive, debilitating, and thoroughly addictive habit. I also know that non-smokers can be, you'll pardon the pun, a pain in the butt.

Aside from kids naïve enough to be conned by the likes of Joe Camel, I don't know a single smoker who's happy about being addicted to nicotine. Most smokers could stand a little sympathy and compassion. What they don't need is some snooty, holier-than-thou zealot preaching at them. Cut them some slack, folks. They're smokers, not lepers.

And if you're really feeling generous, spare a kind thought for

John Taylor. He smoked his last cigarette in the snow outside a public building in Utah.

When he finished his cigarette, Taylor walked back inside the public building, which happened to be the Utah State Prison execution shed. John Taylor was then shot to death by a firing squad.

The state of Utah forbids smoking inside any public building. State murder is still perfectly legal.

Queen Victoria Wouldn't Believe It

Wanna know my least favourite cliché making the rounds these days? It's a one-word expression: "inappropriate."

It's a designation the holier-than-thous among us can use to brand anything they don't personally approve of. A Hollywood movie can be "inappropriate." So can an attitude, the shortness of your skirt, or the length of your hair.

What a prissy, Pecksniffian declaration that is! Cowardly, too. Recently I watched as a high-school basketball coach whistled a stoppage in practice and called a noisy, foul-mouthed student off the court. Looking down his nose (actually, *up* his nose—the kid was really tall), the teacher priggishly announced, "Walter, I find your language inappropriate."

He could have just said, "Stop swearing."

Ah, well, all part of the political correctness crusade, which continues to wash over us. I'd call it a return to the Victorian age, except that would be doing Victorians a disservice. Recent tortured manifestations of political correctness make Queen Victoria look like the proprietress of a bawdy house.

In California, a painting of a nude was recently removed from a public building at the University of Berkeley. Detractors had complained that the portrait "exploits and objectifies women."

It was a print of Goya's *Naked Maja*—a painting that has been considered a priceless classic for the past two centuries.

Oh, well. At least they didn't try to paint a bra and panties on her.

George Washington should be so lucky. You're familiar with that famous painting of Washington by the artist Emanuel Leutz? The one that shows the father of America standing gallantly at the prow of a rowboat while his soldiers ferry him to shore? The painting is called *Washington Crossing the Delaware*, and it's been a fixture in American mythology almost as long as the US has been around.

Alas, thanks to the artist's lubricity, the painting's days are numbered.

Last August, a school district in Columbia, Georgia, recalled 2,300 fifth-grade textbooks. Reason? Well, the textbooks contained a photograph of the illustrious painting, and some sharp-eyed reviewer on the school board noticed that if you squint your eyes almost shut and use your imagination, the pocket watch innocently dangling against Washington's left thigh might be misconstrued by a fifth-grader's eyes as *the Founding Father's penis*.

So the books were recalled, and school-district flunkies spent two weeks assiduously airbrushing the suggestive timepiece out of the picture.

We had an example closer to home recently—in our capital, as a matter of fact. The directors of the Federal Agriculture Museum in Ottawa came down with an interesting variation of mad cow disease. They announced that the giving of feminine names to cows in the museum had been deemed "inappropriate" and would thenceforth be banned.

The reasoning—if it can be called that—was that if a cow named, say, Bessie was being displayed to a school class on a trip to the museum and there happened to be a little girl in the class named Bessie . . . well, she might be embarrassed and humiliated. Particularly if the cow in question happened to be, as a blushing spokesman for the museum put it, "doing certain bodily functions."

Hell, you know how depraved cows can be. Hence the banning of feminine names for cows.

Once the decision was made public, the outcry was so loud that the museum officials hastily changed their minds and rescinded the ban.

Pity. I was dying to know what names they would have deemed appropriate.

Lance the cow, perhaps? Spike? Theodore?

Even cartoons are not immune to the "inappropriate" virus. A recent Disney production featured Donald and Daisy Duck doing a little whitewater rafting. Halfway through the cartoon, their raft upsets and Donald and Daisy are thrown into the river.

And that's where the "standards" board of Walt Disney Enterprises halted the production. They called the animators before them and demanded to know why the characters weren't wearing regulation life jackets.

One of the animators, Robert Gannoway, waited for several seconds and replied in a meek and plaintive little voice:

"Because . . . *they're ducks?*"

Old Levi Would Not Be Proud

I knew it. I could have predicted this would happen from the moment they came out with Stay Prest. You remember that? Levi's Stay Prest? Wash-and-wear jeans. You could climb into 'em as soon as they came out of the dryer?

What a joke. Levi's always *were* wash-and-wear. Only a terminal nerd would consider ironing them. That's the whole point of jeans. Jeans are for people like you and me—and Gilda Radner, who once bragged that she based all her fashion choices on what didn't itch.

Back in the 1960s, the brain trust at Levi Strauss understood that their role in life was to put out a cheap pair of denim pants that would practically stop bullets. Perfect product. And then they tried to finesse. They brought out Stay Prest wash-and-wear—and eventually bellbottoms and hiphuggers and pastels and flare legs and stonewashed and tapers.

This is not what a horny-handed Bavarian merchant by the name of Levi Strauss had in mind back in 1853, when he emigrated to San Francisco.

Strauss was a merchant, an odd jobber who got his hands on a bargain heap of tough, heavy-weight brown canvas. He noticed that the hardrock miners—the famous San Francisco forty-niners—generally wore crummy torn and patched trousers. They need better pants, he thought to himself, and he started cutting up his canvas into trouser patterns—double-seaming the legs, even putting rivets in the stress corners for extra strength. Strauss didn't know it, but he had created the trouser equivalent of the Volkswagen Beetle. His pants were cheap, tough, and terribly common. Just like his newly adopted country.

Strauss gave the pants his first name, and Levi's were off and running.

And run they did. For more than a century, jeans meant Levi's and Levi's meant jeans. During the Second World War, you couldn't even buy them on the open US market. Levi's were strictly reserved for American defence workers. But in the mid-1950s, two things happened to the Levi Strauss image. One was named James Dean, and the other was called Marlon Brando. Their movies—*Rebel without a Cause* for Dean and *The Wild One* for Brando—featured the stars wearing Levi's. The sales went through the roof.

The company could have run with that. It could have kept on turning out merely the best-value pants on the market. But that's not how it works in big business—if it was, we'd still have a six-team NHL.

Nope. By the 1970s, Levi's had become chic. Boutiques all over the world were selling jeans at unbelievable prices. Faded jeans. Patched jeans. Ripped jeans. Even jeans with no knees. In 1973, the president of Levi Strauss admitted that he "found it a little strange to rise from workclothes to fashion, but we're not fighting it."

They should have fought it. Instead, Levi Strauss tried to go high market—opening the door to all manner of foppy foreign designers flogging tissue-thin denim in the most ungodly quasi-polyester mutations. Suddenly, the market was awash in glitzy brands like Gap, Tommy Hilfiger, Big Star, Guess—even Diesel and Gasoline and Kik Girl, for crying out loud.

And somewhere in that swirl, Levi's—like its anagram, Elvis—lost its way.

Really lost its way. In 1998, the one-time giant of the garment trade lost a cool billion dollars. Not long after, Levi Strauss announced the closing of half its twenty-two North American plants.

The buzz on the street? The Levi's people lost it. Tried to be highsteppers, forgetting that they couldn't dance. Their pants just aren't cool any more.

But this is refreshing, because I fell in love with Levi's before they were cool. Back in the 1960s, when only hoods and louts wore them—oh, yeah, and a rumpled, chain-smoking guy by the name of Gzowski, who back in the late 1960s quit as editor of *Maclean's* magazine, announcing that he would never again take a job where he couldn't wear jeans to work.

And he didn't. Got a job at CBC Radio instead, as host of *This Country in the Morning.*

And so I find myself on the high inseam of the millennium: pursuing a work philosophy by Gzowski, wearing a wardrobe by Levi Strauss.

Except that Gzowski is no longer with us. And these Levi's I'm wearing cost more than I paid for my first car.

Plus they're . . . kinda tight.

Black & White and Read All Over

2004

Accordion Guilt

You know supreme guilt? That stabbing pain that is the physical manifestation of remorse and can make you suddenly wince and knit your brow involuntarily?

All of us have something buried in our past that still has the power to make us jackknife upright in bed at three o'clock in the morning.

Let me tell you about mine.

It's been smouldering on my personal back burner for more than twenty years and I need to get it off my chest. My guilty moment involves a seven-year-old niece . . . and an instrument of torture.

It happened sometime around the end of the seventies in the kitchen of my big sister's house not far from Fergus, Ontario. I was young and much cleverer than I am now—clever to the point of smartassedness, actually. My big sister was both older and more mature. She was also the mother of six. Following a delicious home-cooked meal, she announced that her third youngest, Patti, had an after-dinner surprise for us.

Patti scooted away from the table into a back room and eventually reappeared, harnessed and trussed to a piece of machinery that look like a cross between a portable piano and a smithy's bellows, but made out of Formica.

It was, of course, an accordion. I'd seen them before—even heard them—but always at a manageable distance. This one was right in my face. Little Patti started to wheeze out "Beer Barrel Polka." I felt a smile taking over the bottom half of my face. She plunged into "I've Got A Lovely Bunch of Coconuts," and my smile turned into a grin which morphed into a leer.

By the time she was honking out "Lady of Spain," I was cackling uncontrollably, the tears cascading down my cheeks.

It was deeply embarrassing. Little Patti was playing her heart out; others at the dinner table were listening supportively. I was howling like a depraved loon.

I can't help it. Accordions crack me up. I can tolerate bagpipes. I can keep a straight face through a nose flute recital. But accordions just mess my mind.

It's hard to say exactly why. Accordions are hardly the apex of earthly annoyance. Not in a world that includes chainsaws, jock-rock DJs and Margaret Atwood reading her own poetry.

And the instrument is not without its champions. The accordion is the official musical instrument of San Francisco, not to mention Detroit, St. Paul and Skokie, Illinois. Gandhi played a version of the accordion, for heaven's sake. So do Laurie Anderson and k.d. lang.

But on the other hand, so do "Weird Al" Yankovic and the Schmenge Brothers.

I think the soaring accordion IQ (irritability quotient) is due to a combination of things. First, there is the music itself, which is invariably schmaltzy and cloying; and then there's the fact that it emanates from such a ludicrous-looking contraption—one-third keyboard, one-third aircraft instrument panel, one-third mechanical lung—and all of it covered in a glittery Day-Glo veneer. I've got a hunch Elton John's coffin will look a lot like a top-of-the-line accordion.

And of course it is loud. I am always amazed at the sheer gross volume of—well, noise—that an accordion can pump out.

Sounds like a device that should be outlawed along with mustard gas and anthrax bombs, but the accordion does not terrify people, oddly. It makes them smile, albeit uneasily. Or in my case, guffaw maniacally.

I just hope my niece has kicked her accordion habit once and for all. It's not easy. I know of one hard core accordion player who was heading home after playing at a wedding and decided to stop for a coffee. He pulled in at a roadside diner and went inside. He was just sitting down at the counter when he realized—damn!—he had left his accordion in full view in his car! He rushed back to the parking lot, hoping against hope, but it was already too late.

Someone had smashed in his car window and thrown in two more accordions.

But Is It Art?

Does anybody remember what art is? I knew once, many years ago. I was standing in a cave near a town called Altamira in northern Spain. For a few *pesetas*, a local guide had agreed to escort a half dozen of us into an already famous underground grotto decorated with prehistoric paintings. The beam of his flashlight flickered across the cave wall revealing depictions of deer, bison, a few hand prints—and then the guide flicked off the flashlight, leaving us in complete darkness.

After a few seconds he struck a kitchen match and as it flared, he held it close to one of the painted bison.

The bison breathed.

In the dancing flame of the match, the bison seemed to come alive. A few of us actually jumped.

The painting was fifteen thousand years old, put there by a half-naked, illiterate savage who never saw a paint brush, much less a copy of *Gray's Anatomy*, but I did not doubt for a second that it was art. It went straight from the cave wall through my eyes to my heart.

I've never been that sure of a piece of artwork since.

I remember standing in an art gallery in Toronto in front of a metre-and-a-half section of sewer pipe. It was entitled "This is Not a Sewer Pipe" and carried a price tag of five hundred dollars.

One of Canada's most famous living artists is Jana Sterbak. Famous for what? For "Vanitas: Flesh Dress for an Albino Anorectic." It's a sculpture consisting of rib-eye steaks sewn together and left to rot in public.

And I mean public. It was shown at the National Gallery of Canada in 1989.

Or consider the opus of New Yorker David Leslie. Mr. Leslie is a performance artist who thinks "the world needs art that breaks conventions of beauty." That's why his latest artistic statement will take place in a boxing ring. The artist plans to don boxing gloves and protective head gear, then invite anyone in the audience to come into the ring and try to knock him out.

"I'll be covering up," he said, "but people will have, like, fifteen uninterrupted shots at me. It'll be cool."

Then there's the photographic artist Thomas Condon in Cincinnati. He tried to have an art opening consisting of photographs he'd taken in a morgue. Condon had arranged various corpses so that they were holding objects like a syringe, sheet music and an apple. Cincinnati police reckoned it was more like corpse abuse than art, and Condon's been indicted—although a local art critic allowed that "from an art perspective, there is a precedent for [such an exhibit]."

Perhaps the "What is art?" question came full circle at an exhibit in Birmingham, England, recently. The exhibit consisted of . . . nothing. There were no sculptures on the floor, no paintings on display, only stark white walls and a few cardboard signs that read, "Exhibition to Be Constructed in Your Head." An organizer explained that it was "an experiment to see how people react to it."

They want to be careful about encouraging public judgment. They should bear in mind what happened at an avant-garde space called the Eyestorm Gallery in London's trendy West End. Gallery officials opened their doors the morning after a launch party for artist Damien Hirst, only to discover that one of Mr. Hirst's installations had disappeared! Police questioned a building cleaner,

Emmanuel Asare, who readily admitted that when he saw a coffee table littered with cigarette butts, empty beer bottles, pop cans and paper cups, he sighed, swept the whole thing into a garbage bag and tossed it in a dumpster.

When he was informed that he had dismantled a work of art valued at twelve thousand dollars, Asare shrugged and said, "I didn't think for a second that it was a work of art. Didn't look much like art to me."

The world needs more art critics like Emmanuel Asare.

How to Outheckle Hecklers

One of the things I do when I'm not playing hunt and peck with my computer keyboard is speechify. Which is to say I stand up on my hind legs in front of roomfuls of strangers and try to make them laugh.

It's not an unpleasant gig, once you get over stage sweats. Public speakers get to travel all over the country; you meet plenty of folks you otherwise wouldn't, plus you get a nice speaker's fee and usually a free dinner out of the deal.

Of course there is a downside to making public speeches. It is called The Heckler.

It's an uncommon breed, but there only needs to be one of them in an audience of hundreds to ruin a speaker's evening. Contrary to the aura of easy confidence good speakers exude, they're usually sweating bullets up there. Fear of public speaking is the number one phobia, way ahead of fear of heights and fear of snakes. When a speech is going well, the speaker is like a tightrope walker, still scared but getting across. When some buffoon in the third row yells something, it's like having your tightrope wobble. You know you are millimetres away from freefall.

Fortunately hecklers tend to belong to one of two subspecies: stoned or stunned. A drunken heckler usually has just the one arrow in his quiver. Once that's shot, he's roadkill. The stupid ones are more difficult. For one thing, they don't appreciate how stupid they are. Luckily the audience usually does. Audiences, by and large, are incredibly forgiving organisms. They don't like hecklers any more than the speaker does. And if the speaker says something—pretty much anything—that puts the heckler in his place, the audience will rise and cheer as one.

I've never found the perfect squelch for hecklers, but other speakers have handled the situation deftly. Some boob once made the mistake of interrupting David Letterman in mid-monologue. Letterman paused, surveyed the heckler through hooded eyes and murmured, "What exactly is on your mind, if you'll excuse the exaggeration?"

I know a stand-up comedian who skewers males (hecklers are almost always male, and isn't that a surprise?) with "Ah! Good to see you again, back in men's clothing."

If he doesn't feel like toying with the heckler, he dismisses him with "I'm sorry sir, I don't speak alcoholic."

Or, "You'll have to forgive me, I don't know how to deal with you. I'm a comedian, not a proctologist."

And if he's really ticked off, he yells at the heckler, "Save your breath. You'll need it to inflate your date later."

Crude retorts, but we live in crude times. Our ancestors, not surprisingly, handled hecklers with much better grace. The author Charles Lamb was once interrupted during a reading by a heckler who hissed at him. Lamb paused, skewered the interloper with his gaze and purred, "There are only three creatures that hiss: a goose, a snake and a fool. Stand forth so that we may identify you."

Sir Robert Menzies, one-time prime minister of Australia, was once beset at a political rally by a woman heckler.

"I wouldn't vote for you if you were the Archangel Gabriel!" she shrieked.

Menzies calmly replied, "If I were the Archangel Gabriel, madam, you would scarcely be in my constituency."

Ah, but my all time favourite heckler put-down sprang from the lips of a British political troublemaker by the name of John Wilkes. Mr. Wilkes stepped on a lot of toes during his eighteenth-century political career, including a pair of bunioned beauties attached to the Earl of Sandwich. Wilkes and the Earl cordially loathed each other and took every opportunity to so testify. One evening after a boozy dinner, the Earl rounded on Wilkes and thundered, "Egad, Wilkes! I have often wondered what catastrophe would bring you to your end. I think that you shall die of the pox [i.e. syphilis] or the noose."

And quick as a cobra, Wilkes stood up, smiled silkily and retorted, "That would depend, My Lord, on whether I embraced your mistress or your principles."

I'd give up my speaker's fee to get off a squelch like that.

The Ballbearing Invasion

Kids say the darndest things.

—Art Linkletter

They certainly do, and nobody knows it better than the star-crossed professionals who get to spend most of their working hours with our kids—their teachers. Teachers get to mark tests and examinations, and that's where the teachers learn that some kids don't retain information quite as efficiently as others. Hence the student blooper phenomenon. Herewith a collection of some of the more outrageous howlers committed to paper by our little darlings.

Science with a vengeance:

"We get our temperature in different ways. Either fairinheit, cellcius, or centipede."

"One horsepower is the amount of energy it takes to drag a horse five hundred feet in one second."

"A molecule is so small it can't be observed by the naked observer."

Famous people of science don't escape the swipe of bloopism. One student wrote that the law of gravity was passed by Isaac Newton, while another insisted that the Russian Pavlov was famous for studying the salvation of dogs.

Young students seem to have an even shakier grasp of biology.

In a class report one child wrote, "Our biology class went out to explore the swamp and to collect little orgasms." And another juvenile chronicler recorded, "In biology today, we digested a frog."

You want to hope that these kids don't choose a medical career:

"The big artery in your neck is called the jocular vein."

"The pelvis protects the gentiles."

"A permanent set of teeth consists of eight canines, two molars, and eight cuspidors."

"The heart beats faster when you are younger, average when you are middle age, hardly at all when you are old, and not at all when you are dead."

The zounds of music:

"Music sung by two people is called a duel."

"A harp is a nude piano."

"My favourite composer is an opus."

"Agnus Dei was a woman composer famous for her church music."

"A very liked piece is the 'Bronze Lullaby.'"

Putting the litter in literature:

"Shakespeare was famous for writing and performing tragedies, comedies and hysterectomies."

"Shakespeare wrote his plays in Islamic pentameter."

"A great Jewish leader in Scotland was Rabbi Burns."

"I like the story *The Last of the Moccasins*."

"In Ibsen's *Ghosts*, Oswald dies of congenial syphilis."

"Jake Barnes in *The Sun Also Rises* was injured in the groin region and was impudent for the rest of his life."

And then of course there's history, ancient and modern. One student noted that Rome was invaded by the ballbearings. Another explained that the Bolshevik Party was led by John Lennon. And my favourite, a student commenting on fashion in Ancient Egypt:

"Early Egyptian women wore a garment called a calasirus. It was a sheer dress which started beneath the breasts which hung to the floor."

Man, if that didn't make Egyptian guys impudent, nothing would.

Is That a Pig Spleen in Your Pocket?

I want to reassure everyone that this is *not* going to turn into a rant about Environment Canada weather forecasts.

I am *not* going to dwell on the fact that, despite umpteen gazillion dollars worth of thermometers, barometers, anemometers, radar, Doppler, weather balloons and interstellar meteorological satellites, Environment Canada is almost always *dead wrong* about predicting temperatures and conditions in the microclimate that surrounds my house.

I will *not* point out that the Environment Canada spokesperson *never admits* his or her organization screwed up the day after it rains when it was supposed to have been sunny, or when a force-ten gale shows up on what was forecast as a calm day.

I am just going to say that, when it comes to weather forecasting, Gus Wickstrom of Tompkins, Saskatchewan, does it better. What's more, Gus doesn't have a high-tech laboratory full of sophisticated instruments and gauges.

He does his forecasting with pig spleens.

You read right. Gus takes the spleen from a slaughtered pig (older hogs are best), holds it out in front of him, palpates the organ, sometimes even takes a little chomp of it ("I like to bite into it a little . . . I am trying to be more accurate") . . .

And then Gus Wickstrom predicts the weather for Tompkins, Saskatchewan and environs.

Is he any good at it? The *Farmer's Almanac* thinks so. The magazine, which is mildly famous for the accuracy of its own weather forecasts, extolled Gus Wickstrom and his pig spleens in a feature article not long ago. He gets calls from radio stations and TV stations around the continent, asking him to tell the world what the weather's going to be.

He's been interviewed by media outlets in New York and Los Angeles. KOMO TV recently flew him in to Seattle to read his pig spleen prognostications for Washington.

It's amazing what Gus can suss out from a simple pig spleen. "The last few years there's been a blue streak at the bottom of the spleens," says Gus. "That tells me we'll get some rain in May and June. [This year's] spleens have a good layer of fat compared to last year and that usually indicates more moisture."

Is Gus on the money or is he just talking through his porkbellies? Well, last year he went toe to toe with the official Canadian weather office—and mopped the floor with them.

"Environment Canada has thousands and thousands of dollars worth of equipment," says Gus, "and last year they said it would be cold and wet [in the Prairies].

"But the spleens showed exactly the opposite, and that's what we got—a warm and mild winter with little precipitation."

Environment Canada has a bit of an excuse in this contest—they've only been around for a few decades. Spleen-reading goes back for generations.

"It came from my dad's side of the family," says Gus. "They came to Saskatchewan from Sweden back in the early nineteen-hundreds. But weather predictions with spleens were done in Stockholm long before that."

Gus has great respect for a body organ that doesn't get a lot of positive press, generally speaking. He says the spleen is a powerful piece of meat that can do much more than tell you if it's going to rain on your parade. He says slapping a chunk of raw spleen on your balding head promotes hair growth.

"I often wear it under my hat when I go to check the mail," he says. He's a big fan of taking spleen internally too. Gus reckons a feed of spleen is good for folks with rheumatism, arthritis, bad hearing, failing eyesight.

"It can put a little zip in your life," he says. Speaking of which, Gus cautions against eating too much spleen. He says a little under 120 grams a day is the absolute maximum. Why? Because spleen is . . . well, as Gus said, powerful.

"It acts like Viagra. Anyone can eat it—men or women—but there is no use only one spouse eating it since that person will overpower the other."

Aha.

That explains that famous old Prairie expression: "Is that a pig spleen in your pocket or are you happy to see me?"

A Fewmet by Any Other Name

Birds do it, bees do it.
Even educated fleas do it . . .

—COLE PORTER

When deer produce 'em, they're called fewmets. When they come from otters they're called spraints. For dogs, the proper word is scumber, and for seabirds, guano. Even paleontologists have a special name for them. When they find samples produced by a dinosaur and fossilized by the ages, they call them coprolites.

I am referring, in case you haven't guessed, to poop.

Considering its commonality to all species, doo-doo doesn't get nearly the respect it deserves. Some species almost don't do it at all. The Guatemalan jumping viper hits the outhouse but once a month, while the average rabbit unloads about every three minutes.

Humans? Well, as you and I and the folks who make Exlax and the folks who make Kaopectate know only too well—it depends. If it makes you feel better, Sigmund Freud was constipated for the better part of his life, which probably explains that pained expression he wore. Good job Freud wasn't Italian. Mussolini was deeply suspicious of constipation. He considered it a symptom of latent communism, and ladled out copious doses of castor oil to anyone he considered a "carrier."

Other famous figures have ascribed great powers to common poop. The philosopher Pliny prescribed hippopotamus droppings as a cure for epilepsy. (Used in a poultice? Ingested? Do we really want to know?) Michelangelo slathered donkey dung on his statues to give them that aged look. Hippocrates swore by pigeon poop scalp massages as an antidote to baldness.

I have known hairlessness and I have known pigeon droppings. I believe I'd rather be bald.

Aside from quack remedies, has the stuff ever done us any good? You bet. Natives on our prairies depended on "buffalo chips" for fuel. For centuries China has used human excreta extensively for fertilizer. And some say that Australians never would have had organized agriculture if they hadn't imported millions of tonnes of guano to make their soil fertile.

Unidentified droppings have had their moment in the military side of world affairs as well. Back in the late seventies, when the United States was mired in a particularly deep swamp of doo-doo called the Vietnam War, newscasts and newspapers were suddenly full of speculation that the wily Viet Cong were launching chemical warfare attacks. The proof? Huge swathes of southeast Asian jungle foliage spattered with little yellow spots. It showed up on tanks and tents and even soldiers' helmets. US military advisors announced that it was "yellow rain," possibly a virulent, contagious form of deliberately spread chemicals and a complete violation of the Geneva Convention.

Actually it was bee poop. At the height of the monsoon season, bees in some parts of the tropics take wing in vast swarms, soar toward the heavens and engage (for reasons known only to bees) in a ritual of mass defecation.

Some interpreted it as a hymenopterous commentary on the stupidity of warfare, but whatever the cause, there was an alarming amount of bee guano about.

Which brings up the fascinating concept of volume. Some tiny microbes don't produce enough to register on a microscope slide, while the blue whale offloads up to three tonnes daily. On the plains of Serengeti in Africa, it's estimated that wildebeest herds leave behind four thousand tonnes of personal calling cards.

Per day.

Speaking of volume, let's have a moment of silence for the German zookeeper who, just a while back, lost his life in the elephant enclosure of a zoo in southern Germany.

Seems the chap had just finished administering a laxative to a badly constipated bull elephant. Then he made the fatal mistake of walking around the stern of the beast at precisely the moment that the laxative . . . took effect. Death was attributed to a combination of shock, asphyxiation and full-body trauma.

Of all the times to be caught without an umbrella.

Snowball the Dog

This is a story about a dog. A dog that belonged to a friend of mine in Thunder Bay some moons ago. A story I'm sure my friend would prefer to see buried deeper than a dog bone for all time. I have no wish to drag my friend or his canine into the limelight unnecessarily. So I'll just call him . . . Jim.

Hyder.

Jim thought it would be grand to get his little six-year-old daughter a puppy for Christmas. He thought it would be even grander if he took her with him to the Thunder Bay animal shelter so that she could pick out the pup herself.

With the benefit of hindsight, I'm sure Jim would agree that that was his first major blunder.

"I want the white one," chirped Laura. "The one eating the cinder block."

They took the white one. Laura named it Snowball. According to the animal control officer it was a husky, though if I'd had to guess, I would have leaned toward albino wolverine. Snowball was a certified hellhound. Mike Tyson should have had Snowball. Snowball made pit bulls look like pantywaists.

Not that Snowball was vicious. Just strong willed. Accent on the strong.

Laura could never take Snowball for a walk on a leash—she'd have been dragged to her death. Hell, even when Jim took him he looked like a water skier behind a runaway cigarette boat.

And then there was Snowball's appetite. Snowball was basically a fur-covered black hole. He gnawed chair legs. He shredded throw rugs. He ate whole couch cushions. He gulped, for God's sake, a three-hundred-gram tin of goldfish food—tin and all. He horsed his way through mountains of dog kibble and, without missing a bite, continued to eat the plastic dish that held the dog kibble. Snowball ate like he'd never been fed. Which was a problem. Jim was a single parent with a steady job. He couldn't leave Snowball outside all day, not in a Thunder Bay winter. But neither could he give him free run of the place. Not if he didn't want to come home to a hovel that looked like a Bronx crack house after a raid. So what Jim did—he loaded Snowball's food bowl, filled his water dish and locked him in the bathroom for the day. What could a dog do in a bathroom, eat the tub?

No. But he ate the toilet seat, demolished two towel bars and, Jim swears, scarfed half a dozen Bic razors.

One day Jim came home to find—it was springtime now—Snowball, who had been locked in the backyard, sitting happily with a powdery white moustache festooning his muzzle. Snowball had discovered, chewed open and devoured a bag of toxic rose dust—you know that poisonous stuff you put on rose bushes to kill bugs? Jim hurried to the shed to get the garden spade, hoping he could dig the hole, toss in the carcass and get the dirt tamped down before his daughter got home from school. Snowball just watched, snacking on the odd nugget of gravel Jim threw up. He didn't die from the poison. He didn't get sick. Jim swears that Snowball didn't so much as burp.

The dog was an indestructible, bottomless dynamo. When neighbourhood kids started throwing broken toys, plastic water bottles, even a two-metre fluorescent skipping rope into the back-yard—laying bets on how long it would take Snowball to devour them—Jim knew the dog had to go.

He put an ad in the paper: "Free dog to a good home." Or maybe he didn't even specify good. The ad was answered by a Little

Old Lady. She, unaccountably, loved Snowball. The last Jim saw of the dog it was stampeding down the sidewalk, the Little Old Lady joined by the wrist, trailing out behind like a human streamer.

Another Jim—James Thurber—once wrote, "If I had any belief about immortality, it is that certain dogs I have known will go to Heaven. And very, very few persons."

Well, that's as may be. But if I ever get there and I spot a white dog cocking its leg against the Pearly Gates . . .

I'm gonna look St. Peter in the eye and say, "Cancel my reservation."

Body Double Trouble

To the perfectly lovely young woman who approached me in the grocery store this morning: I'm sorry. I apologize. I was neither drunk nor off my medication.

To everyone who wasn't at the grocery store this morning, here's what happened.

I'm standing in the produce section looking for a ripe cantaloupe among the mottled bowling balls before me when suddenly this woman—this total stranger—comes waltzing up the aisle and says, "Hi. Remember me? From the party last week? I'm the one who just moved into Howard's house."

Number one: I don't know any house owner named Howard. In fact I don't even know any indigents named Howard.

Number two: I know perfectly well that I haven't been to any parties recently.

To sum up: I have no idea who this woman is or what she's talking about.

So how do I handle the situation? I do what I always do when someone I've never met engages me in a totally meaningless conversation. I lie.

"Oh, right!" I say. "The party—great party! How could I forget? That's a swell house you've moved into too!"

Why do I behave in this shameful and dishonest fashion? For one thing, the old noodle isn't quite as whipcrack sharp as it used to be. I don't have grey matter upstairs, I have Swiss cheese. I sometimes forget a face. Hell, I sometimes forget entire families. So when I get into a conversation with a (possible) stranger, I pretend I'm with it in order to play for time, on the off chance that I just might remember something.

The other—and more important—reason I feign comprehension is that I have a brother. A brother who is, ahhh, somewhat less mature than I, to be sure. A brother who is obviously not nearly as dashing or charismatic, but a brother who, aside from some totally superfluous cranial fur, looks a lot like Yours Truly.

The fact is, people get us mixed up. A lot. So people often yack away at him under the impression they're conversing with his more elegant brother or vice versa. And since we only live a few kilometres apart, it happens often.

As luck would have it, I ran into my brother downtown just an hour after the grocery store incident.

"Happened again, bro!" I said. "Some wacky woman came up to me in the store, swore she met me at some party. Said I'd remember her because she's living in Howard's place."

He looked at me a little oddly.

"That was Sidney Shannon," he said. "You met her at Molly's birthday party last week. You talked to her for half an hour, spilled your wine on her and ate all the shrimp off her plate."

Oh . . . yeah. Molly's birthday party. It's coming back now.

So anyway, my apologies, Sidney. Just a touch of amnesia brought on by the old war wound. And while I'm in a confessional mood, that guy at the party who tried to make you wear a lampshade and sing "Barnacle Bill the Sailor" with him?

That was my brother.

The Incredible Disappearing Cellphone

Got on the bus the other day and sat down across from a guy who was cleaning his ear. Gross, I thought. Then I realized he was also talking to himself, or rather, to his wrist. Which is when I clued in; I'm a slow learner. The guy was simply using his cellphone.

In a public place, in a loud, obnoxious voice, telling the rest of the passengers way more than any of us wanted to know about his abysmally boring day job—but that's another rant.

No, the point I want to make here is that his cellphone was so small there was a danger of it getting lodged in his ear. Why are cellphones getting so damned tiny?

Years ago—and not that many, come to think of it—cellphones were the size of bread loaves. They were huge, ungainly things you could use for a doorstop. Granted they were ugly and cumbersome, but I think we've gone too far in the other direction. Cellphones today are so diminutive they fold down to about the size of a business card.

Which would be fine except for one drawback: physiology. God is still turning out human models with the same size of hands. Those hands include fingers that were never designed to hunt and peck through a cellphone number pad that's not much bigger than a postage stamp. I note that one cellphone manufacturer is now offering a pointy little stylus that fits over the end of your dialling finger, allowing you to punch one button at a time instead of three.

We doan need no steenkin' stylus . . . what we need is a human hand-sized number pad.

And it's not just cellphones. The same thing applies to PDAs, handheld electronic games and hotel radios. Ever tried to change the station or set the alarm on the bedside radio in your hotel room? Who are those things designed for, leprechauns?

The communications business is going nuts over miniaturization right now, and it's getting dangerous. If you don't believe me, ask Antonio Mendoza of Los Angeles. Mr. Mendoza, an attorney at law, has just been released from his local medical trauma centre, following the successful removal of his cellphone from his, er, rectum.

"My dog drags the thing all over the house," he explained. "He must have dragged it into the shower. I slipped on the tile and sat right down on the thing."

Bad enough, right? How would you like to explain to the admissions nurse why you needed to see a doctor pretty quick? But the story gets worse. It took doctors more than three hours to perform the extraction, because the cover to Mr. Mendoza's phone had opened during insertion.

That's right. Throughout the operation, Mr. Mendoza was . . . getting calls.

"He was a real trouper during the entire episode," said one doctor. "Three times during the extraction the phone rang, and each time, he made jokes about it."

Mr. Mendoza is back at work now, walking a little gingerly, but otherwise none the worse for wear. Obviously, he's a resourceful, outgoing, fun-loving guy—if a tiny bit clumsy.

Just don't ask him to turn the other cheek.

Computers and Poetry? Why Not?

There's a guy in my town named Herc. He is shortish but extremely muscular. Think human fire hydrant. The word on Herc is: don't mess with him. Oh, he's friendly and gregarious enough, most times. But he's also as tough as a platoon of Ninjas, and if you incur his wrath, your allotted span on this planet can be measured in nano-seconds.

Which is why it was unusual to see Herc lined up at the local Libation Emporium one day, grinning like a man who'd won the Lotto 6/49.

"You're looking mighty chipper today, Herc," said the checkout clerk. "What's up?"

Herc smiled a smile as wide as the Liberal Party deficit and said, "Just walked down to the end of the bleepin' dock"—Herc swears a mite—"with my bleepin' computer, an' I hove that bleeper as far as I could inta the harbour.

"And it felt so bleepin' good that I went back home, got my printer and I hove that motherbleeper in after it!"

I know exactly how Herc feels. I love my computer when it's doing what I want it to do. Which would be about one-point-three percent of the time.

The rest of the time I hate my computer. I hate it more than

Eaton's hated Simpson's. More than Alberta hated Trudeau. More than Tyson hated Holyfield.

If I could find an ear on my computer I would gnaw it off.

But I can't. I can't find much of anything on my computer. That's the point.

I could probably live with my handicap if only my computer wasn't so bleeping smug. I'll be working away on it when suddenly my monitor screen will go into a kind of graphic stomach cramp and a message will flare across the screen: "This program has performed an illegal function and will be shut down."

What? What illegal function? I paid for this computer! I'm over twenty-one!

Another favourite computer moment occurs when I painstakingly type in some incredibly stupid Internet address—(htttp://LiZard~xanadu/medusa/@#&phrymzik.com)—the computer clicks and whirrs, and this message pops up on my screen: "Could not connect to [1.135.245.49].

"Cause: connection timed out. (10060)"

Gee, thanks, Bill Gates. I can sure work with clear and concise info like that.

No point in appealing to your friendly neighbourhood computer geeks. They understand this gobbledygook! It makes sense to them! Nope, folks, we're on our own.

Well . . . maybe not quite.

I hear that the honchos at Sony Vaio Programming in Tokyo have replaced the stupid and meaningless Microsoft error messages with . . . haiku poetry. Which my dictionary defines as: a very short Japanese style of poetry, consisting of three lines.

And how does that apply to computer error messages? Try these:

A file that big?
It might be very useful
But now it is gone.

First snow, then silence.
This thousand dollar screen
Dies so beautifully.

A crash reduces
Your expensive computer
To a simple stone.

And my personal favourite:

Windows XP crashed.
I am the blue screen of death.
No one hears your screams.

Computer programming with a sense of literature *and* a sense of humour? What next? Macintosh?

A Bug in Your Ear

The *Globe and Mail* headline blared the news: "Cellphones Safe, U.S. Study Finds." Scientists have determined that cellular telephones don't give users brain cancer after all.

My first reaction was: damn! I'd been pulling for the brain cancer option. Anything that might slacken the death grip of that single most invasive and obnoxious morsel of modern technology.

I know, I know. The cellphone is a godsend for marooned mountaineers, stranded motorists and anybody who can't come up with two bits for a pay phone. But when did it become mandatory for everybody with an index finger to pack one? The damn things are everywhere. For a while I thought the streets of my town were home to a mass epidemic of earaches. People were all walking around with one hand jammed to the side of their head. Then I realized they were on cellphones.

People can't seem to just walk or sit in contemplative silence anymore. They have to call somebody. Right now. And it's only going to get worse.

Check the local schoolyard. Little prepubertal schoolkids cling to their cellphones as if they were locks of Britney Spears' hair. As a matter of fact, that relates to the latest application for the cellphone; it's become a pop concert accessory. Kids take their Nokias and Motorolas to performances by their favourite stars, and in the middle of the show they whip them out, dial up a friend and wave the cellphone at the stage so that their non-ticket-buying friends can experience the next best thing to being there.

Pretty spooky, but if a couple of Frankenstein wannabes over in the UK have their way, Cellphoneworld will soon become even spookier.

Two researchers affiliated with the European partner of the Massachusetts Institute of Technology have come up with what they call the audio tooth implant, also known as the molar mobile or the telephone tooth. It is a tiny receiver that can be implanted in one of your back teeth. The device allows the patient, hereafter referred to as the schmuck, to receive phone calls, listen to music, even connect to sound sites on the Internet, directly on a back molar which then transmits the audio signal through the jawbone to the inner ear.

The inventors aren't just targeting brain-dead, headbanger teenagers. They reckon the device will be popular with investors and brokers, not to mention sports fanatics desperate to follow the play-by-play of their favourite teams around the clock.

The brainiacs behind the telephone tooth haven't figured out a way to make outgoing calls, but, given the breakneck pace of technology—cellphone wasn't even a recognized noun twenty years ago—it's only a matter of time.

I take solace in the fact that the term cellphone rage is growing even faster than cellphone mania. Innocent bystanders are finally standing up and yelling back at the ignorant yackers and jabberers in our midst. A woman on a BC ferry was recently yapping into her cellphone in the middle of the lounge when a fellow passenger said in a loud voice, "Madame, I think I speak for the other passengers here when I say we don't care to hear about the gossip from your office, so please finish your call or take it out on the deck."

Cellphone resentment in Toronto runs even higher. Doctors at Toronto General report treating mobile phone talkers for black eyes and even in one case, a cracked rib, all results of cellphone rage.

The actor Lawrence Fishburne stopped in midperformance during a Broadway play last year, fixed a member of the audience with a glare and bellowed, "Will you turn off that (expletive) phone, please?"

He got a standing ovation.

Speaking of standing, that's what I was doing in a highway restroom recently, minding my own business when a voice floated over the wall of the cubicle next to me.

"Hi," it said.

"Hi," I answered uncertainly.

There was a pause, then the voice said, "What are you doing?"

"Well," I stammered, "I'm just making a pit stop, I'm travelling west on the highway, just like you are, I guess."

There was an even longer silence. Then the voice said, "Look, honey, I'll call you back. Some idiot at the urinals is answering every question I ask you."

Cellphones. I hate 'em.

Pitch Black

2005

Going to Pot

Did I ever tell you about the time I impersonated a cop?

Relax, sergeant—it was several years ago, in another provincial jurisdiction. I lived in the sticks at the time, the hour hand had long passed midnight and some party-hearties in a house down the road were making noise. Way too much noise.

I took it for an hour and a half and then I called the cops. A bored dispatcher informed me that, as it was the weekend and due to budgetary cutbacks, no police were actually on duty, but an officer could be summoned from a nearby jurisdiction "in an extreme emergency."

I was younger then, with a shorter fuse and not nearly the level of urbanity and decorum for which I am so justly renowned today. Accordingly, I slammed down the receiver, said some bad words, put on my police hat and loaded my police dog into my cruiser. Together we drove down the road and fetched up in the driveway of the aforementioned party house.

A word about my cruiser, my police hat and my police dog.

The "cruiser" was an '82 white Ford station wagon. Something Ned Flanders might drive. The police hat was a nylon mesh cap I picked up after a charity softball game between a rural police detachment and the radio station I worked for. (Over a post-game beer, the cop who played shortstop informed me he coveted my CBC ball cap. We swapped.) The crest on the front of my new cap read "Ontario Provincial Police, South Porcupine." Not exactly a slogan calculated to strike fear into the hearts of evildoers, but a collector's item, I felt.

My "police dog" Rufus was in truth a mangy border-collie-and-indeterminate-mix mutt, but I hoped that in the dark and from a distance he might pass for an on-duty Alsatian.

I hammered on the front door, which was ajar, walked in, and in my best Lorne Greene voice of doom boomed, "WE'VE HAD SEVERAL COMPLAINTS ABOUT THE NOISE YOU PEOPLE ARE MAKING. IF YOU CAN'T TONE IT DOWN, I'M GONNA HAVE TO LAY CHARGES."

What I did was totally illegal, not to mention surpassingly stupid. But it worked like a charm. Know why?

Because it was a pot party, not a booze party. The joint reeked of . . . well, joints. And as I delivered my sermon, people all over the room were surreptitiously divesting themselves of baggies, stubbing out roaches, palming ashtrays and trying desperately not to exhale in my face.

What's more, they were all stoned. Instead of seeing me as the ridiculous impostor I clearly was, they were figuring that the dope they were smoking was unusually excellent.

Know what would have happened if that had been a booze party instead of grass fest? There's a good chance I would have been stomped into a carpet stain. And I'm not exaggerating. That very fate befell a lawyer in Squamish, BC, not long ago. He went to a booze party at a neighbour's house to ask people to pipe down. Two of the knuckle-dragging juiceheads in attendance kicked him to death.

All of which is a long-winded way of getting to my point, which is: why the hypocrisy about marijuana?

Recently, the federal New Democrats did backflips to distance themselves from their leader Jack Layton's rather brave endorsement of the substance. Politicos of other stripes (yellow) puffed themselves up to solemnly intone how they'd never touched the stuff—and who can forget Bill Clinton's pathetic cavil: "I smoked, but I didn't inhale"?

Well, I did, Bill—and what's more, I don't know of more than half a dozen adults who haven't tried pot at least once. It's no big deal, folks. Let's finally admit it.

Am I advocating pot for everyone? No. I don't smoke it anymore because it's too expensive, not worth the hassle and it makes me stupid. It also makes me hungry and lazy—two conditions I have enough trouble grappling with when I'm clear-headed.

All I'm saying is, let's stop being two-faced about it. Booze causes a thousand times the grief, bloodshed and property damage that pot does, but we turn a blind eye because through a fluke of justice and thanks to the twisted principles of seedy old perverts like J. Edgar Hoover and Alberta's own Emily Murphy, alcohol is legal and marijuana isn't.

The Canadian legal system is woozily staggering toward righting this absurdity, but it's not there yet, so think twice or even three times before you flout the law, even if the law is, to paraphrase Dickens, a demonstrable ass when it comes to a backyard weed.

But if you must smoke—keep it down. Don't make me put on my police hat and come over and bust you.

Danger! Hugs Ahead

Well, I've been living in the Gulf Islands for ten years now—which doesn't exactly give me bragging rights, but it does put me in a position to offer a cultural observation or two.

Such as: What's the big deal, anyway? What's so different about living on Pender Island compared to Penticton? Cranbrook compared to Galiano? Sicamous compared to Salt Spring? If somebody blindfolded you and dropped you off in, say, downtown Ganges—how would you even know you were on a Gulf Island?

Well, it's very simple. If you are on a Gulf Island, sooner—rather than later—someone will come up and hug you.

Don't ask me why. I spent most of my life ricocheting across Canada, getting by on nods, winks, waves and handshakes—and not being hugged all that much, aside from close family and (all too rarely) consenting members of the opposite sex.

But the very first person I met when I got to Salt Spring wrapped me in a big, smothering bear hug.

And he was my real estate agent.

And we're not talking that fake Hollywood kiss-kiss, squeeze-squeeze fabulous dahling, microhug, no. Gulf Islands hugs are heartfelt, wholesome, solemn and . . . long-ish. Your Gulf Islands hug can last longer than a Todd Bertuzzi cross-checking minor.

The classic Gulf Islands hug, which is as formal and ritualistic as a coronation at Westminster Abbey, goes like this. Hugger and huggee advance toward each other until they are deeply into each other's personal space. Beatific smiles, though not mandatory, are recommended. Both parties slowly throw arms wide and glide in for the clinch. As full frontal contact is made, all four arms close rapturously in maximum hug mode while, simultaneously, each party's chin goes over the other's right shoulder. Eyes should be closed at this point. If beatific smile is not in place, a look of intense bliss is acceptable.

This pose is maintained in total, ecstatic silence for minimum thirty seconds, after which both parties smoothly swivel heads backward and to the right, bringing chins to rest on each other's left shoulder. Hold and marinate meaningfully for at least half a minute.

This is the formal conclusion of the Gulf Islands hug.

Both parties can now step back and speak normally. "Hey, Kevin, how's it goin', eh? D'ja get your garage shingled yet?"

Needless to say this is all deeply bewildering for most visitors to the Gulf Islands—and for some islanders too. Like me. I'm of Scottish ancestry. We don't hug. Not without a lot of . . . well, Scotch.

But, that's the way it is—and it could be worse. Last summer we had a guy came back to the island after spending five years in LA. He was Mr. Cool. With the diamond earring. The white linen jacket. The Converse sneakers with no socks.

He was sashaying down the bar at Moby's giving high fives to everybody, slapping palms. Doing that hippy-dippy thumb-clutch thing where you grab the other guy's thumb and kinda saw back and forth like you're bucking up firewood . . . When he got to me, he put out his fists for that ultrahip fist-bump that morphs into a game of one potato, two potato. But I was too fast for him. Quick as a flash, I grabbed him in a bear hug and held him 'til he came to his senses.

Cruel? Hell no. My turf, my rules. Come to the Gulf Islands, you're gonna get hugged. It's the law.

Confessions of a Carnivore

Went to a huge lobsterfest last week. Dozens of the bristly brutes had been express air-freighted in from PEI and boiled on the spot. Not surprisingly the place was packed with enthusiastic diners armed with forks and pincers, drooling onto their bibs. They weren't disappointed. Everybody got a hulking two or three-pounder hanging off both sides of the plate.

Except me. I settled for the potato salad, some sliced tomatoes and two buns.

It's not that I'm a vegetarian or even lobster-phobic; it's just that I prefer the food on my plate to be a little more gullet-ready. Any time you catch me with a pair of pliers in my hand and wearing a drop sheet, chances are I'm on my way to change the oil, not eat a meal.

On second thought, *do* put me down as lobster-phobic. I don't know what heinous crimes those creepy crustaceans committed in their previous karmic life but it must have been grim to look as evil as they do. Lobsters are indisputably ugly suckers, whether they're scuttling across the ocean floor or reclining on bone china. It's not your average life form that can manage to appear flamboyant and hideous at the same time. Lobsters look like steroid-pumped cockroaches in drag.

And there's the labour component. When you sit down to a lobster dinner, you don't just dig in; you have to deconstruct them first. You're not eating a meal—you're conducting an autopsy.

What really turns me off is that a lobster on the plate is so blatantly a creature lately deceased. Porterhouse steak is not like that. Neither are pork chops or chicken breasts. I'm more comfortable when the biological origins of my food are camouflaged. How many of us could cheerfully tuck into a lamb kabob if it arrived at our table looking remotely like the loveable, bleating, gambolling cutie it so recently was?

Hypocritical? You bet. Hypocrisy is the operative mode for your twenty-first century human carnivore. After all, very few of us kill, gut and dress our own meat these days, and a lot fewer of us would be carnivores if we did. I know, for once, whereof I speak. As a teenager I worked at the Ontario Public Stock Yards. I was an alley rat—a cane-waving middleman between the farmers who brought in their livestock and Canada Packers, the purchasers who, ah, "rendered" the beasts. I guarantee that if most Canadians spent one afternoon in a slaughterhouse, we would be known as a nation of lettuce eaters.

But we don't choose to put ourselves through that. Instead we buy our meat at the supermarket or the delicatessen, nicely sawn up, sculpted and vacuum-packed into amorphous portions like so many protein pucks. Oh, we won't eat absolutely *anything*. We wrinkle our noses at Europeans who eat horse and Indonesians who eat dog, but is that so very far removed from our taste for veal or squab? Aren't we just talking about different menus?

Me, I'm a most unlikely carnivore. I don't hunt. I don't fish. I even rescue spiders from the bathtub and relocate them on the woodpile by the side door. And yet I eat meat. How do I justify that? I don't. I just do it. I pretend that what's on my plate was not recently excised from a dewy-eyed Aberdeen Angus or a frolicking Dorset lamb. I just close my eyes, shut down my mind and chew.

Mind you, I would renounce my guilt-ridden habit and give up meat tomorrow, but for one thing.

It tastes so damn good.

I tried living without meat once. I was a vegetarian for two years.

I inhaled more green than a Mastercraft lawnmower and sucked back more pasta than Pavarotti. But the gastronomic limitations got me in the end. I discovered that the lowly soybean curd is lowly for a reason. And a man can eat only so many zucchini-goat cheese casseroles.

I respect and admire the old vegan adage about not eating "anything with a face." I just can't live up to it, that's all.

Just call me a reluctant carnivore. And a two-faced one, at that.

Feeling No Pain

I don't recall all the comic books I devoured in my misspent youth, but I do remember one of them. It was called *Haunted Tales* and it specialized in creepy stories calculated to send shivers of dread down impressionable prepubescent spines.

I even remember one particular story in *Haunted Tales*. The first panel showed a close-up of a delicious-looking chocolate bar, still in its shiny wrapper, lying on a dock by a lake. Along comes a middle-aged-looking guy with a fishing rod over his shoulder, obviously out for a day of angling. He spies the chocolate bar, picks it up, unwraps it and pops it in his mouth with a contented smile.

In the next panel he's dropped the fishing rod and his eyes are as big as golf balls. His mouth is all puckered and distended—and now you can see a thin, taut line running from the corner of his mouth straight across the dock and into the water. The fisherman is on his knees and he's being dragged—reeled in—inexorably across the dock. The last panel of the story is a close-up of the lake surface with just a few bubbles rising and the fisherman's hat floating beside them.

The story was a rather clever, if unlikely, morality play designed to make the reader think about angling from a different . . . angle, as it were. The moral being, "What if fish did to us what we do to them?"

Except . . . not.

Anybody who's ever hooked a fish—be it a sixty-pound tyee or a six-inch chub—knows that what you have right from the get-go is A Fight. The fish struggles, resists, tries with every muscle in its body to shake that hook out of its jaw.

Now imagine yourself in place of that fish on the line, with a great big treble hook set deep in your cheek. (And imagine that, like a fish, you have no arms to grab the line and relieve the pressure.) Would you be shaking your head and bucking your weight against the hook? No. You would be whimpering and mincing and tippy-toeing ever so rapidly in whatever direction the hook was pulling you. That's because we human beings have oodles of nerve endings in our cheeks. A hook in the cheek would hurt plenty.

Whereas fish—at least in the bony cartilage of their mouths—have no such nerve endings. That's why they can put up a fight when they're hooked.

Now I know I'm going to get letters on this—especially from the PETA folks. PETA—that's People for the Ethical Treatment of Animals—has already spent millions of dollars on a campaign to outlaw angling, which it considers barbaric.

All I can say is, save yourself a stamp.

Get in touch instead with James D. Rose at the University of Wyoming. As a professor of zoology and physiology, he's been working on the ins and outs of fish neurology for the past three decades. Recently Professor Rose published a study that compares the nervous systems of fish and mammals. His conclusion? Fish lack the brainpower to sense pain or fear.

But a minnow sees a largemouth bass coming at him and flees—isn't that fear? No, says Professor Rose, that's nociception—responding to a threatening stimulus. Which he contends is an entirely different kettle of . . . well, you know. According to Professor Rose's report, the awareness of pain depends on functions of specific regions of the cerebral cortex that fish simply do not possess.

So it looks like PETA's out of luck with their anti-angling crusade—but wait a minute! What about bait? Doesn't live bait suffer from cruel and unusual punishment?

Not necessarily. I remember the time I was ice fishing on a lake north of Thunder Bay. It was bitterly cold, and I wasn't getting a nibble.

Just then an old Finlander settles in about thirty yards away, bores a hole in the ice, drops in a line and starts hauling in fish after fish. Finally I can't stand it. I walk over to him and say, "Excuse me, but I've been here all day and I haven't had a bite. You've been here half an hour and you've got a dozen on your string. What's your secret?"

"Roo raff roo reep ra rurms rarm," he says.

I say, "Sorry, I didn't catch that."

"Roo raff roo reep ra rurms rarm."

I say, "Sounds like you're speaking Finnish—can you tell me in English?"

With a look of disgust he spits a slimy brown ball into his mitten and says, "You have to keep the worms warm!"

Cycle Psychology

The bicycle has done more to emancipate women than anything else in the world.
— Susan B. Anthony

A woman needs a man like a fish needs a bicycle.
— Irina Dunn

It's been a long and somewhat bumpy ride for the familiar two-wheeler. Baron von Drais started it all. Away back in 1817 the eccentric German hammered together a contraption that became known as the Draisienne. It was made of wood, with wheels, a seat and handle-bars but no pedals. In order to ride the Draisienne, you had to shuffle your feet along the ground. The Draisienne did not go platinum.

A couple of decades later a Scotsman by the name of Macmillan improved on von Drais's hobby horse. He added swinging cranks on the front wheel which were connected to rods and levers to the back wheel. The whole thing was made of iron and weighed about sixty pounds. It too was something less than a bestseller.

In 1870 the first real bicycle, the penny farthing, was invented. It got its name from the difference in size between the wheels—the front wheel looked like a big English penny, the back wheel like a tiny farthing. It took a lot of skill to stay upright on the penny farthing and even if you did the ride was bone-crushing, thanks to the solid tires.

By the time I came along, which is to say firmly nestled in the glut of post-World-War-II baby boomers, the bicycle makers pretty much had it right. Their new improved product was light, the tires were filled with air, the seats were soft and the pedalling, thanks to a chain drive, was easy.

I still remember my very first bike. It was a blue-and-white CCM one-speed with a leather seat and a push bell screwed to the handlebars. Why, I cut my teeth (my shins and knuckles, actually) on that piece of technological wizardry.

State of the art. Yep, by the middle of the twentieth century, bicycles had gone about as far as they could go.

We thought.

No one was aware of it, but the winds of change were already licking at the kickstands of the bicycle world as we knew it. One day Tommy Farmer rode into the schoolground pedalling what might as well have been a UFO. It was a racing bike with drop handlebars and brakes mounted on the handlebars right next to a little gizmo none of us had seen before.

It was a chrome-plated Sturmey-Archer gearshift with a tiny lever you could move with your thumb. Imagine! A bicycle with three speeds—first, second and third! Suddenly the rest of us felt like we were riding Draisiennes.

But of course it was only the beginning. Europeans invented derailleurs which led to the creation of five-speed bikes and then ten-speed bikes. The concept of getting off and walking a bike up a steep hill became almost unthinkable.

And even that was the Dark Ages. In the 1980s, some bike boffin came up with the idea of adding cogs to the rear gear cluster. Suddenly bikes appeared with fifteen, eighteen even twenty-one and twenty-four gears. Mountain bikes appeared—ungainly hulks with great nubbly tires and complicated suspension systems. Serious cyclists debated the relative merits of brakes from Japan, sprockets from Italy and featherweight magnesium-alloy toe baskets from

Czechoslovakia. My first bike, mint-fresh from the CCM factory, set my dad back a whopping $29.95. Today you can pay more than that for a pair of cycling gloves—and they won't even have fingers.

Or if you really want to wow your cycling friends the way Tommy Farmer wowed us way back in the fifties—buy yourself an Urbanite.

You can order one from Urbane Cyclist, a shop in Toronto. Urbanites sell for $750 per and they are cutting-edge trendy, with great colours, happening handlebars, a way cool imitation-leather saddle . . .

And oh, yes—no gears. The Urbanite is a single-speed bike, just like the ones the kamikaze bike couriers ride in the big city.

Just like the old CCM I learned to ride on half a century ago, as a matter of fact.

No difference really.

Aside from the $720.05.

The War Between the Sexes

Men and women, women and men. It will never work.

—ERICA JONG

There's a brand new babysitting service available in Hamburg, Germany. For ten Euros—that's about eighteen bucks Canadian—housewives bent on shopping can drop off their charges at the Nox Bar in downtown Hamburg. The deposit buys the women a few uninterrupted hours in the shops and boutiques, while their "responsibilities" are treated to two beers, a meal and unlimited televised sports on the big screens mounted over the bar.

Obviously we're not talking about the ladies' offspring here. We're talking about their mates. Men hate shopping, and women hate shopping with a grumpy spouse in tow. Solution: park him in a sports bar and everybody's happy.

It's a kindergarten for grownups—male grownups specifically. It's also a graphic illustration that men indeed are from Mars, women are from Venus and seldom will their intergalactic orbits intertwine.

We really are different, you know. Screw all that Alan Alda, sensitive-caring-male bushwa. Men and women are like the poles of a magnet—constantly pushing in equal but opposite directions.

My partner recently went away on a trip for ten days. I knew there'd be trouble when she got back. Sure enough. Not two minutes in the door and she's muttering about a few empty pork and bean tins on the kitchen counter, whiskers in the bathroom sink and a high-tide mark on the bathtub that looks like one of the rings of Saturn. Talk about neurotic.

It pains me to say this, but women just aren't very practical. Why should I make the bed every morning when I know perfectly well I'm just going to have to unmake it at the end of the day? What's the point of wasting a valuable resource like hot water to do dishes morning, noon and night when I can just let them pile up and do them all in one marathon session Saturday afternoon? Okay, Saturday afternoon and evening? Why doesn't *everyone* hang his undershorts on the lampshade if he knows he's going to wear them the next day? It makes them easy to find, plus they're warm when you put them on.

In any case, it's not my fault. I have an untreatable medical condition. I'm a man. That means that, besides having two or three gender-specific anatomical doodads, I am mentally programmed differently from women. All men are, according to Michael Gurian. He's a social philosopher and he's just published a book called *What Could He Be Thinking?: How a Man's Mind Really Works*.

Gurian says my brain simply doesn't take in sensory details as efficiently as a woman's. In other words, it's not that I'm a slob, I literally do not *see* that smear of peanut butter on the fridge door or yesterday's balled-up sweat socks draped across the chesterfield.

I'm at a chemical disadvantage too. Gurian claims that the male brain secretes only a tiny dribble of a powerful bonding chemical called oxytocin. Women's brains are awash in the stuff. Oxytocin deprivation explains why men shy away from touchy-feely conversations. Also why most of us would prefer a prostate exam conducted by a doctor wearing a hockey glove over the ordeal of sitting through one edition of *Oprah*.

And oxytocin isn't the only chemical we get shortchanged on. Gurian says men also produce less serotonin than women, which is why we need more of what he calls "mindless" distractions to relax, like "Monday Night Football" and Schwarzenegger flicks.

Does Gurian expect his book to change male pattern dumbness? No, he sees no future there. His book is an attempt to help women better understand the Homer Simpson in their life. "Men get this already," says Gurian. "They are living this brain, but they don't have the conscious language to explain it."

Oh, I don't know. I thought George Burns nailed it pretty good. He said, "There will always be a battle between the sexes because men and women want different things.

"Men want women and women want men."

Wheelbarrows and Chickens

There's a famous poem called "The Red Wheelbarrow" by William Carlos Williams. It goes:

*So much depends
upon*

*a red wheel
barrow*

*glazed with rain
water*

*beside the white
chickens.*

The poem is famous, I think, because in just sixteen words, it sums up the ineffable magic of the here and now. I like to think of Williams—he was a country doctor in New Jersey as well as a poet—walking across a farmyard one morning, black bag in hand, perhaps after assisting at a childbirth or sewing up some hired hand's cut leg, coming around the corner of a chicken coop, seeing the wheelbarrow and the chickens and being transfixed by the . . . perfection of it all.

It is a poet's gift—and task—to discover the magnificent in the mundane. For most of us it takes a bigger jolt than the sight of a wheelbarrow and a clutch of chickens to be reminded of the preciousness of each moment. But the world is still brimming with strange and miraculous happenings that ought to take our breath away if we're paying attention.

Consider the story of an unusual six-year-old boy named James Leininger of Lafayetteville, Louisiana. James loves airplanes—particularly World War II airplanes. Always has. Once when he was out shopping with his mother, he pointed at a toy airplane. His mother remembers, "I said to him, 'Look, it has a bomb on the bottom,' and he told me, 'That's not a bomb, it's a drop tank.' I had no idea what a drop tank was."

James Leininger did. He was two and a half years old at the time.

James's fascination with airplanes continued. He played with nothing but toy airplanes and even dreamed about them. Then the dreams became nightmares. "I'd wake him up and he'd be screaming," his mother recalled. "I'd ask him what he was dreaming about, and he'd say, 'Airplane crash on fire, little man can't get out.'"

Gradually, the little boy's memories became more specific. He "remembered" that he flew a plane called a Corsair. "They used to get flat tires all the time," he said. He "remembered" that his pilot name was also James. Once his mother asked him what happened to him in the Corsair. "Got shot," he said. Where? "Engine." Where did it crash? "Water." Who did it? "Japanese." How did he know? "The red sun on the plane."

One day his mother made meat loaf for dinner—something she hadn't made since before James was born. Little James looked at his plate and said, "Meat loaf! I haven't had this since I was on the *Natoma*."

Natoma? Neither parent had ever been involved in the military or aviation. The only aviation-related items in their house were James's toy planes. Where was the kid picking up this stuff? His father Bruce began to investigate. He searched the internet, combed through military records and discovered that during World War II a US aircraft carrier called the *Natoma Bay* was stationed in the South Pacific. Twenty-one of its crew died during the Battle of Iwo Jima, including a Corsair pilot named James Huston. On the afternoon of May 3, 1945, witnesses saw Huston's plane take a Japanese hit to the engine. It crashed into the sea and sank.

Young James doesn't have the nightmares anymore and his memories are fading as he grows older. But the story isn't fading, it's growing. Bruce Leininger contacted the families of the twenty-one crew members who died in the Battle of Iwo Jima. All of them spoke of "a spirit" visiting them in the years since the war.

And they all want to meet young James Leininger. This year, his parents plan to take him to the *Natoma Bay* veterans' reunion.

So is it a crock? I suppose it could be. Professor Paul Kurtz, a paranormal investigator at State University in New York thinks so. He says the parents are "self-deceived."

"They're fascinated by the mysterious and they've built up this fairy tale," he says.

Could be. And perhaps a red wheelbarrow is just a red wheelbarrow.

Accustomed As I Am

Guess which single activity scares more people than anything else in the world. More than falling off a mountain or being lost in the jungle or getting stuck in an elevator with Sheila Copps, even.

Making a speech. Specifically, standing up on one's hind legs in front of a roomful of strangers and putting one's mouth in gear.

It's an odd phobia when you think about it. You're not treading water in a tank full of hungry hammerheads. Nobody's waving a blowtorch over your nether regions. What's the worst thing that can happen when you get up to make a speech? You start to hiccup? You discover your fly is open?

Actually it can be much, much worse than that. As a guest speaker, I've been standing up and mouthing off to rooms full of strangers for the past twenty-five years. I've speechified to doctors in Toronto, lawyers in Vancouver, building contractors in Florida and Canadian soldiers in Germany—not to mention sanitation workers in Sudbury and prospectors in Flin Flon, Manitoba. I've heard the words "Ladies and gentlemen, please welcome, Arthur Black . . . " hundreds and hundreds of times.

And yes, I still get butterflies in the belly before I speak.

But mine is not the irrational fear of the toastmastering tenderfoot. I come by my nervousness honestly. After all, I was once guest speaker at a convention of Canadian meat packers.

They are a robust confederacy, your meat packers. Indeed, an occupation that consists of poleaxing large animals, dismembering them and rendering their body parts into shrink-wrapped gobbets on Styrofoam trays is unlikely to engender a brotherhood of effete and hypersensitive aesthetes. These particular meat packers were rowdy, rude and profanely huge, with thighs like wharf pilings and forearms like beer kegs.

And those were the wives.

What's more, they had been golfing all afternoon, fortifying their performance on the links with lusty belts of rum and flagons of beer dispensed, I was informed, from a golf cart specifically designated as a travelling saloon.

They were, in short, drunk. And the open bar at the back of the convention hall suggested that they wouldn't get sober any time soon.

It is never a good idea to give a speech to a roomful of drunks. But it's a profoundly bad idea to give a speech to a roomful of drunks who have been genuinely entertained by a speaker just before you.

In this case I was preceded by a stand-up comic who was—I swear I'm not making this up—stone blind. Not only blind, but paralyzingly funny. This guy gingerly tap-tapped his way up to the microphone with his white cane—and then he laid them in the aisles. The audience loved him. He was very, very funny.

Then it was my turn. "HERE'S ANOTHER GUY GONNA MAKE YEZ LAUGH!" thundered the emcee, grabbing me by the sleeve and hurling me toward the microphone.

I didn't. Perhaps they'd squandered their entire empathy quotient on the blind comedian or maybe I was overpoweringly mediocre that night, but they didn't laugh. Not once. They drank, they mumbled, they looked at their watches and yawned and scratched, but they did not laugh.

My speeches normally run about forty-five minutes. My speech to the Canadian meat packers went on for seven and a half years, it felt like. Near the end I was sweating and shouting hoarsely to be heard—I think they were very close to rushing the stage and beating me up—then, like a bad dream, all the noise in the room stopped for one moment. No one coughed, no one scraped a chair and, for a nanosecond, I stopped reading. Total silence.

And into that silence floated the voice of a woman in the audience—not loud, but perfectly audible to everyone in the room. And what she kind of . . . murmured . . . into that moment of crystalline silence was:

"Why doncha shaddap and siddown, ya asshole?"

Yes, I thought to myself. Why don't I? And I did.

It was easily the worst night I've ever spent on a stage, but it was also perversely liberating. I had crossed a horror threshold. After the meat packers, no audience has held much terror for me.

But making a speech is never a complete cakewalk, nor should it be. Tension drives all things vital, be they violin strings, vocal chords—or that electric void between a speaker and his audience. One day you, dear reader, will be called upon to bridge the gap between a lectern and some strangers in a darkened hall, armed only with your tongue and your wits. Here are some tips that will make your ordeal easier.

Use technology. Print out your notes in at least sixteen-point type, bold faced and double-spaced. Nothing's more daunting than glancing down at a page of your own pithy observations only to see what appear to be randomly scattered carapaces of tiny insects.

Avoid alcohol. Okay, one small glass of wine, but that's it. Any more and you run the risk of coming off too loud, too slurred and too dumb.

Pack heat. Always keep at least one all-purpose zinger in your quiver to defang hecklers. When one drunk kept interrupting comedian Steve Martin, he paused, put on a bemused look and said, "Oh, yeah. I remember when I had my first beer . . . "

I've always been fond of the deceptively withering, "Thank you. We are all refreshed and challenged by your unique point of view."

Observe the three Bs: be audible, be brief and be seated. And the greatest of these is brevity. No audience ever complained that a speech was too short. The best advice I ever had about public speaking came from a laconic Finlander who asked me to "say a few words" to a roomful of Rotarians in Thunder Bay many years ago.

"But Einar," I hissed as he pulled me to the stage, "what should I speak about?"

Einar looked at me and muttered, "Speak about three minutes."

Elvis a Scot? Gude Laird!

To paraphrase the late, great Friendly Giant, I want you, dear reader, to look up, waaaaaay up. All the way up to the tippy-top northeast corner of Scotland, there to espy the wee village of Lonmay, not far from Aberdeen.

Okay? Now I want you to look back, waaaaaaay back, to the year 1745. See that burly fella with the Popeye forearms heading out of town with all his worldly possessions in a gunnysack and a one-way ticket to North America sticking out of his pocket?

That would be Andy—Andy of Lonmay to his friends. He's emigrating to America—to the American south, in fact—where he will continue his vocation as a blacksmith, gradually sand down his Scottish burr to a Mississippi drawl, and make his seminal (literally) contribution to one of the great legends of the twentieth century.

It's all foretold in the family name Andy is painstakingly printing in block letters for the ship's manifest: "Presley."

You're looking at Andrew Presley—the great-great-great-great-great-great-great-grandfather of Mr. Rock 'n' Roll, Elvis Aron Presley.

At least that's the way Alan Morrison figures it. He's written a book called *The Presley Prophecy* and he claims he's traced Elvis's roots back eight generations—right to August 27, 1713, when the father of the aforementioned Andrew Presley tied the knot with one Elspeth Leg in Lonmay, Scotland.

Elspeth? Sounds like someone with a lisp trying to say "Elvis," does it nae?

If Morrison is right, that means Elvis's blood type is indisputably tartan.

Elvis a Scot. Gude Laird, have we not done enough damage? Scots have already given the world plaid, curling, oatmeal, Argyle socks, haggis, kilts and bagpipes. Will the abuse never end?

Blasphemy, you cry? Nonsense. I speak as a descendant of a long line of lowland sheep molesters. The "Blacks" whose name I carry were members of an obscure sect of the MacGregor clan. Why "Black"? Who knows? Maybe some of my ancestors were blacksmiths like Andy Presley. Or perhaps we specialized in chimney sweeping. Possibly we were a band of rogues whose full name was Blacksheep. Or it could be we just practised spectacularly poor personal hygiene—I don't know. It doesn't matter. Even though I am almost as far removed from the heather-clad hills as the King himself, my lineage is undeniable. I am—och, aye—a Scot.

The genealogical evidence may be lacking but I can feel it in my bones. I actually like porridge, for God's sake. I watched the Briar last winter. And the slightest skirl of the bagpipes sends a tingle through my carcass, closely followed by the insane desire to mount a suicidal charge—if not on a German machine gun nest, at least upon the tone-deaf hell hound playing the pipes. Only a descendant of the inmates on the far side of Hadrian's Wall could betray such a chequered pedigree.

Of course, I jest—and that's Scottish too. In this alum-sphinctered, hyper-politically correct world in which we live, it would be worth my life to make such ethnically disparaging jokes about Muslims, Italians, Comanches, Bosnians, Nigerians or Québécois—but jokes about Scots? Hey, take your best shot. We are the human piñatas of stand-up comedy. The last ethnic group you can safely laugh at.

Why? Because we can take it. My people are as obstinate as Scotch broom, as sturdy as Scotch pine, as hearty as Scotch broth and as tenacious as Scotch tape.

We are also reputed to be somewhat on the thrifty side. I can't confirm or deny the charge, but I will relate the tale of my great-uncle Harry and his visit to London some years ago. Uncle Harry got on a city bus, tucked his suitcase under the seat and said to the conductor, "Tower of London, please."

"That'll be 60p plus 10p for the suitcase," said the conductor.

"What?" said Uncle Harry. "I'll no pay for my suitcase!"

"If you don't pay for the suitcase," said the conductor, "I'll throw it off the bus."

Uncle Harry refused. The conductor picked up the suitcase and pitched it straight out the door—right into the River Thames.

Uncle Harry was outraged. "You English crook!" he roared. "You're not satisfied with trying to rob me, you're trying to drown my wee lad as well!"

Hair Today and Gone Tomorrow

. . . the law, sir, is a ass—a idiot.

If anyone needed visual confirmation of the words Charles
Dickens put in the mouth of Mr. Bumble, one need go no
farther than a typical British courtroom during a typical British
trial. There you might watch one of Britain's most eminent barristers mellifluously declaiming subtle and abstruse points of law
in soaring language with Shakespearean flourishes and Miltonian
profundity.

And he will be dressed like a geriatric drag queen.

British barristers wear robes and wigs. Have done since the
seventeenth century. And I don't mean understated Frank Sinatra
hairpieces or sleek Captain Kirk toupées—the wigs the Brits wear
are mangy, white pageboy bobs, made out of horse hair, crudely cut,
heavily powdered and heavy as sin.

Sure, they made a dynamite fashion statement back in the sixteen hundreds, but nowadays—why? Traditionalists argue that the
wigs and robes help instill respect for the law.

Yeah, right—but why not go for something lighter and more
contemporary, like Groucho Marx glasses and a Ronald McDonald
clown suit?

Ah, well. Men have always been a little loony in the head hair department. I haven't got as much mileage (or hair) as Rumpole of the Bailey, but I've lived through brush cuts, boogie cuts, Elvis pompadours, ducktails, Afros, Beatle cuts, Mohawks, buzz cuts and the Mel Gibson mullet.

I don't want to come on like I'm cutting-edge trendy when it comes to hair, but—well, I *am* cue-ball bald. And that, my friends, is the latest hot look for gents—no hair at all.

And not just on the head. Have you seen Arm & Hammer's latest cosmetic come-on? Nair For Men.

The male-targeted hair removal gel has been selling briskly down south for a while now. According to a survey released by the company that manufactures the stuff, 30 percent of American males between the ages of eighteen and thirty-four regularly shave off their chest hair.

When did this start? I thought the hairy-chested he-man was the standard all ninety-pound-weaklings aspired to.

Ah, but that was before Ah-nold. As a body-builder, Governor Conan proved that you could have a chest as bare as a baby's bum and still look like a walking bag of walnuts.

According to scientists, Schwartzetcetra and his hair-removing imitators may simply be responding to a biological imperative. Researchers at Oxford and Reading universities suggest we humans originally shed our furry primate pelts half a million years ago to protect ourselves from disease-carrying parasites.

"Smooth skin has therefore become an evolutionary calling card we use unconsciously to pick healthy mates," says Sir Walter Bodner, an Oxford University spokesman.

Admittedly, those guys you see at the beach in thongs and what looks like a welcome mat growing on their backs probably aren't sexual turn-ons for anybody this side of a lowland gorilla in heat. Still I think I'll cling to what's left of my body hair.

My beard, I mean—particularly after what happened to my pal Arvid. He was down at the local barbershop getting a shave last week and he mentioned the trouble he has getting a smooth shave around the cheeks.

"Got just the thing," said the barber, taking a small wooden ball from a nearby drawer. "Before you shave, just put this in your mouth between your cheek and your gum."

So Arvid tries it. He pops the ball in his mouth, it makes his cheek puff out, and sure enough—the barber proceeds to give him the closest, smoothest shave he's ever experienced.

"This ib grape, Al," says Arvid, trying to talk around the ball, "but what happens if I swallow it?"

"No problem," says the barber. "Just bring it back tomorrow like everyone else does."

Acknowledgements

The content of *Black Gold* has been selected from:

Basic Black (Penumbra, 1981)
Back to Black (Methuen/CBC Enterprises, 1987)
That Old Black Magic (Stoddart, 1989)
Arthur! Arthur! (Stoddart, 1991)
Black by Popular Demand (Stoddart, 1993)
Black in the Saddle Again (Stoddart, 1996)
Black Tie and Tales (Stoddart, 1999)
Flash Black (Stoddart, 2002/Harbour, 2004)
Black & White and Read All Over (Harbour, 2004)
Pitch Black (Harbour, 2005)